Cambridge O Level

Biology

Revision Guide

Second Edition
Ian J. Burton

CAMBRIDGE
UNIVERSITY PRESS

CAMBRIDGE
UNIVERSITY PRESS

University Printing House, Cambridge CB2 8BS, United Kingdom

One Liberty Plaza, 20th Floor, New York, NY 10006, USA

477 Williamstown Road, Port Melbourne, VIC 3207, Australia

4843/24, 2nd Floor, Ansari Road, Daryaganj, Delhi – 110002, India

79 Anson Road, #06–04/06, Singapore 079906

Cambridge University Press is part of the University of Cambridge.

It furthers the University's mission by disseminating knowledge in the pursuit of education, learning and research at the highest international levels of excellence. Information on this title: education.cambridge.org

© Cambridge University Press 2000, 2015

First published 2000
Second edition 2015
20 19 18 17 16 15 14 13 12 11 10 9 8 7 6 5

Printed in Great Britain by CPI Group (UK) Ltd, Croydon CR0 4YY

A catalogue record for this publication is available from the British Library

ISBN 978-1-107-61450-5 Paperback

Table of Contents

Chemicals are moved around living organisms. Here there is a description of the movement of water, ions, sugars and amino acids within a plant (involving transpiration and translocation). This is followed by a description of the human circulatory system and of the constituents of blood.

Introduction – sets the scene of each chapter, helps with navigation through the book and gives a reminder of what's important about each topic.

Carbohydrates

These are organic chemicals containing the elements **carbon, hydrogen** and **oxygen** only. The ratio of atoms of hydrogen to atoms of oxygen in a carbohydrate molecule is always 2:1 (as in water – hence carbo**hydrate**).

Carbohydrates with large molecules such as **starch** and **glycogen** are insoluble (a starch 'solution' is in fact a starch suspension).

Important terms – clear and straightforward explanations are provided for the most important words in each topic.

NOTE

The cytoplasm and the nucleus make up the *protoplasm.*

Notes – quick suggestions to remind you about key facts and highlight important points.

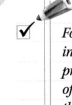

✔ *Fold a leaf (e.g., Lantana) in half, so its upper surface comes into contact with itself, then tear the leaf along its fold. With practice, you should be able to leave a thin, transparent piece of lower epidermis along one side of the fold. Carefully remove this and transfer it to a drop of water on a microscope slide. Gently lower a cover slip onto the specimen, and using low power on your microscope, identify the guard cells. You may need a higher power to see the chloroplasts within the guard cells.*

Task boxes – check your own knowledge and see how well you're getting on by answering regular questions and doing activities.

Aim:	**To show that light is necessary for photosynthesis**
Apparatus:	• a well-watered, de-starched, potted plant (for example, *Pelargonium* or *Coleus*)
	• a cork cut into two pieces
	• a pin

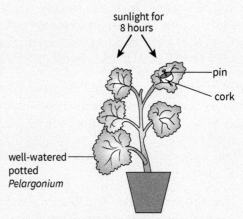

Method: The apparatus is set up as shown in Figure 2.2. The cork is fixed in the evening so that the leaf has time to destarch over night.

The experiment is left in sunlight for 8 hours. The cork is removed from the leaf, and the starch test is carried out on the leaf.

Results: Where the cork covered the leaf, the leaf stained **brown**. The rest of the leaf stained **blue/black**.

Figure 2.2 Experiment to show that light is necessary for photosynthesis

Conclusion: Only where light had been able to reach the leaf had starch been made; thus, light is necessary for photosynthesis.

Practical skills – reinforce your practical knowledge and skills with clear explanations and diagrams.

Points to remember

* Know the similarities and differences between plant and animal cells.
* Know the difference between **tissue, organ** and **organ system** and be able to define each.
* Be able to define **diffusion** and **osmosis**.
* Learn what is meant by **active transport**.
* Be able to write down definitions of the following terms: **plasmolysis, turgor, water potential, partially permeable membrane**.

Points to remember – at the end of each chapter so you can check off the topics as you revise them.

Exam-style questions for you to try

1. What is meant by the term 'dual circulation'?
   A. A blood cell passes through the heart twice in one complete circulation.
   B. Blood travels twice round the body before being pumped to the lungs.

Exam-style questions – thoroughly prepare for examinations by completing the exam-style questions and checking your answers which are provided at the back of the book.

Revision Guidelines

Understanding Biology at Cambridge O Level is not usually a problem, but committing facts to memory can often be a major obstacle to success. Many students are at a loss to know exactly how to set about what seems to them to be a task of immense proportions. I offer the following method, one which I devised myself when, as a student, I was faced with the same problem. It has the advantage, if followed carefully, of improving one's factual knowledge as a result of time spent, rather than of any specific effort to learn.

All important words, terms and phrases in the text of this book have been written in bold and italics. The greater the amount of material thus presented in the text that is committed to memory, then the greater the chances of success in examination. The method which I offer for learning it is as follows:

1. Take a sheet of file paper and divide it with a vertical line such that three quarters of the sheet is on the left of the line.

2. Read a page of the Revision Text, and each time you come to a word or phrase which appears in bold and italics, then construct a simple question to which that word or phrase is the answer.

3. Write these simple questions on the left-hand side of your sheet of file paper, leaving a space between each, and number them. Continue on further sheets of paper if necessary.

4. If there is a diagram in the text, then draw a quick sketch of the diagram on the left-hand side of your sheet with numbered label lines above each other extended towards the right-hand side of your sheet.

5. When you have reached the bottom of the page of text, close the book and see how many of the answers you can write down on the right-hand side of your sheet. When you have attempted all answers, check them against the text. You will probably be surprised at how well you do, but since you wrote the questions, carefully phrased around the required answer, perhaps it is not so surprising after all.

6. Continue until you have a list of questions and answers to the section you are trying to learn.

7. Take a second sheet of paper (folded if writing would otherwise show through it), and use this to cover the answers. Test yourself again, writing your answers on the folded sheet, and continue this until you are able to score over 80%. (You can, of course, set your own target. Some will not be content until they can score 100%.)

8. File away your Question/Answer sheet for further revision at a later date.

9. Continue this process systematically, until you have, effectively, a full set of revision notes for later use.

10. In the last few weeks before an examination, it is better to revise by reading the text of this book carefully, a chapter at a time. Concentrate on every sentence, making sure you understand what you have read. It is so easy to get to the bottom of a page in a book, and realise that your mind was elsewhere as you were reading it, and as a result, nothing registered at all. If that happens, be honest with yourself. Go back to the top of the page and start again.

11. In the last few days before examination, your Question/Answer sheets should now prove invaluable for last-minute consolidation of your facts.

It cannot be stressed too strongly that examination results depend on knowledge. It is important that you have a very good grasp of simple knowledge to do well and interpretation questions often rely heavily on a sound knowledge of the subject matter.

The advantage of this revision method is based so firmly on the student phrasing the questions to which he or she will already know the answer that it would defeat the object if more than a short example of the technique were given. The success of the method relies only on the student following the technique carefully. It does work, but you must be prepared to spend the necessary time. You may even enjoy the experience!

Example

Example of a Revision Sheet, based on the beginning of Chapter 1 in this Revision Guide (Cell Biology), is shown here.

1. What word is used for organisms containing only one cell?	unicellular
2. Give an example of a one-celled organism.	a bacterium
3. What word is used for organisms made of many cells?	multicellular
4. What structure controls the passage of substances into and out of a cell?	cell membrane
5. In what state must all chemicals be before they can enter or leave a cell?	in solution
6. What is the jelly-like substance where chemical reactions occur in a cell?	cytoplasm
7. What is the correct term for the chemical reactions in a cell?	metabolic reactions
8. Whereabouts in a cell are chromosomes found?	the nucleus
9. What do chromosomes contain?	genes
10. Of what chemical are chromosomes made?	DNA
11. What makes up protoplasm?	cytoplasm + nucleus
12. What is the space in the centre of a plant cell?	vacuole
13. What does this space contain?	cell sap
14. What is the name of the box in which a plant cell is contained?	cell wall
15. What chemical is this box made of?	cellulose
16. Name the green structures in photosynthesising cells.	chloroplasts
17. What pigment do they contain?	chlorophyll

18–23. Add the labels to the diagram.

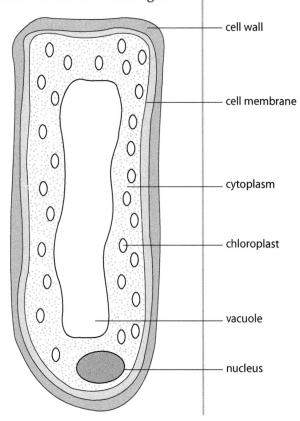

cell wall

cell membrane

cytoplasm

chloroplast

vacuole

nucleus

In addition to producing a revision sheet, it will help to commit facts and concepts to memory if, while studying a topic, you stop occasionally to discuss or to solve a related problem. Biology is a subject that encourages a student to conduct investigations to supplement their knowledge and understanding. Throughout this text, there are 'task boxes' indicated by a tick (✓) to the left of a pencil point. The tasks fall into three categories: category 1 is a simple mental task that will allow you to see whether you understand the topic under consideration. If you are unable to answer any question asked in the task box, you may consider discussing it in a small group, arriving at an answer and then checking, either with a text book or teacher, to see whether you are correct. Categories 2 and 3 will help to supplement you knowledge of a topic. Category 2 is in the form of a simple practical exercise that can be carried out on your own, while category 3 may be more suited to a practical investigation that might be carried out as a class exercise or demonstration.

Some hints on how to draw biological specimens

Drawing specimens is not an exercise in artistic ability; it is an exercise in **observation**. Your drawings should therefore show the features that you have observed.

* Your drawings should be as large as the paper you are drawing on will allow.
* They should be made using a **sharp**, preferably HB, pencil.

* They should have **sharp outlines** (not 'sketchy' ones).

* They should have the same **proportions as the specimen** you are drawing. If the anther is, say, three times wider than but only one-sixth as long as the filament, it should be drawn as such. Measure the specimen before you begin and make very faint marks on your paper to guide you. (They can be carefully erased afterwards.)

* If there is a clear point of structural detail in the specimen – e.g., nectar guides on the petal – the same points should be shown on your drawing, in the correct place. (If they are a large number of similar such points, only a few need be drawn.)

* Avoid shading. If an area is darker than the rest of the specimen, draw an outline of the area and label it.

* **Rule** label lines in pencil and label in pencil preferably in capital letters (pencil can be rubbed out and corrected, and capitals are usually easier to read). Label lines should terminate **exactly at the point being labelled.**

* Avoid arrowheads on your labels – they can obscure an important feature beneath them.

* Always give a **magnification** to your drawing. It is a **linear** magnification, i.e. calculated by measuring the length or width of the specimen, and the length or width of your drawing measured across the same structural feature.

$$\frac{\text{length of drawing}}{\text{length of specimen}} = \text{magnification (expressed as, e.g., '× 4.5')}$$

NOTE

When drawing from a photograph, there is sometimes a magnification given for the photograph. In such cases, you must multiply the magnification of your drawing by this figure.

It would not normally be the case that your drawing or measurements would be accurate enough to give a magnification to more than one decimal place. Do not 'round off' too much. × 4.6 is not × 5.

As an examination approaches and a greater amount of time is spent on revision, it is usually more productive to set aside a certain time each day for revision. Do not allow yourself to be persuaded to do anything else during that time.

Work on your own with **no distractions around you**. Some people say they can work better listening to music. If that really is so in your case, then keep the music quiet, and, at least, it may shut out other distractions!

You may find it helpful to make a calendar by dividing a piece of paper into a space for each day during your revision period before any examination. Then you can divide the syllabus into the same number of parts as there are days for revision, and enter one such part per day on your calendar. In this way you will know exactly what you are going to revise on each day. Your day's revision will not be complete until you have revised everything on your calendar for that day.

People vary as to how long they can work at a stretch. It is important to have a break from time to time (again, preferably, the same time each day). When you stop, set yourself a time to resume your revision, **and stick to it**.

Finally, good luck with your revision. This method can work. I know, because it did so for me!

Ian J. Burton

Acknowledgements

Every effort has been made to trace the owners of copyright material included in this book. The publishers would be grateful for any omissions brought to their notice for acknowledgement in future editions of the book.

Syllabus Name & Code	Paper & Question Number	Month/Year	Chapter/Page in Book
Cambridge O Level Biology 5090	Paper 22, Q1	November 2011	Chapter 1, P 25
Cambridge O Level Biology 5090	Paper 21, Q8	November 2010	Chapter 1, P 26
Cambridge O Level Biology 5090	Paper 22, Q2	June 2011	Chapter 2, P 57
Cambridge O Level Biology 5090	Paper 22, Q6	November 2011	Chapter 2, P 58
Cambridge O Level Biology 5090	Paper 22, Q7	November 2011	Chapter 3, P 76
Cambridge O Level Biology 5090	Paper 02, Q3	June 2008	Chapter 5, P 126
Cambridge O Level Biology 5090	Paper 22, Q8	June 2011	Chapter 5, P 126
Cambridge O Level Biology 5090	Paper 2, Q1	June 2007	Chapter 6, P 164

Reproduced by Permission of Cambridge International Examinations. Cambridge International Examinations bears no responsibility for the example answers to questions taken from its past question papers which are contained in this publication.

The authors and publishers acknowledge the following sources of copyright material and are grateful for the permissions granted.

Cover Mehau Kulyk/SPL; p. 3 Marshall Sklar/SPL; p. 4 Kevin & Betty Collins, Visuals Unlimited/SPL; p. 5 Dr. Robert Calentine, Visuals Unlimited/SPL; p. 6 Dr David Furness, Keele University/SPL; p. 8 Melba Photo Agency/Alamy; p. 35 Jubal Harshaw/Shutterstock; p. 35 Dr Keith Wheeler/SPL; p. 137 Dr Jeremy Burgess/SPL; p. 138 Susumu Nishinaga/SPL

SPL = Science Photo Library

1 Cell Biology

In this chapter, cell structure is considered, as well as the importance of the cell as a basic component of all living matter. Various adaptations of a cell are discussed together with the adaptations that a cell can undergo in order to perform different functions. The methods used by cells to absorb chemicals are described, as is the action of enzymes which are chemicals released by cells.

Cell structure and organisation

The basic unit of life is the **cell**. The simplest living organisms have **one** cell only. Such organisms are described as **unicellular**.

Bacteria (singular: bacterium) are examples of unicellular organisms.

Most other living organisms have many cells, and are described as multicellular.

All cells have the following structural features in common.

1. A **cell membrane**, which **controls** the passage of substances into and out of the cell. One of the most important of those substances is **water**. All other substances which pass do so **in solution**. Since larger molecules are unable to pass through the cell membrane, it is described as **partially permeable**.

2. **Cytoplasm**, a jelly-like substance in which the chemical reactions of the cell (**metabolic** reactions) take place, and which contains the nucleus.

3. The **nucleus** contains a number of **chromosomes** largely made of the chemical DNA. Chromosomes possess **genes**, which are responsible for programming the cytoplasm to manufacture particular proteins.

When a cell divides, it does so by a process called **mitosis**, during which each chromosome forms an **exact replica (copy)** of itself. The two cells formed are thus identical both with themselves and with the original cell.

Plant cells have the following additional structures (Figure 1.1):

1. A (**large, central**) **vacuole**, which is a space full of **cell sap** (and, thus, sometimes called the **sap vacuole**), which is a solution mostly of sugars. It is separated from the cytoplasm by the **vacuolar membrane**.

NOTE

The cytoplasm and the nucleus make up the protoplasm.

NOTE

DNA stands for deoxyribonucleic acid.

NOTE

Plant cells undergoing cell division do not have a vacuole.

NOTE

Cellulose is a tough, insoluble carbohydrate.

1

NOTE

Magnesium is a necessary component of the pigment chlorophyll.

2. The **cell wall** is a 'box' made of **cellulose** in which the cell is contained.

3. **Chloroplasts** – only if the cell is involved in the process of **photosynthesis**. These are small bodies lying in the cytoplasm. They are green in colour because of the pigment **chlorophyll** which they contain.

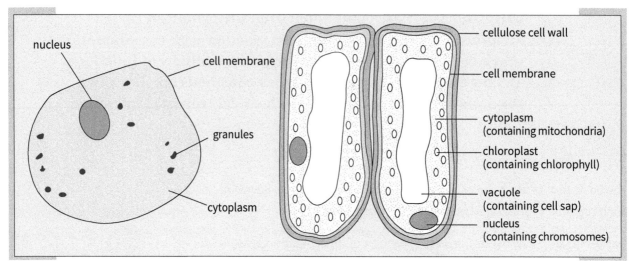

Figure 1.1 Animal cell (liver) and plant cells (palisade mesophyll cells from a leaf)

NOTE

Since, in plants, the cell membrane fits tightly against the cell wall, it is not usually easily visible.

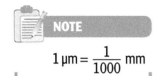

NOTE

$1 \, \mu m = \dfrac{1}{1000} \, mm$

Similarities and differences between plant and animal cells are shown in the table below:

	animal cell	plant cell
similarities	cell membrane	
	cytoplasm	
	nucleus	
differences	no sap vacuole	sap vacuole
	no cell wall	cell wall
	no chloroplasts	may have chloroplasts
	never stores starch	may store starch
	around 10–20 μm in diameter	around 40–100 μm in size

Aim: To observe animal cells

1. Cut a cube of *fresh* liver, in section, approximately 1.5 cm square. (Frozen liver is not suitable as freezing damages the cells.)

2. Scrape one of the cut surfaces of the cube with the end of a spatula (the end of a teaspoon would do).

3. Transfer the cells removed to a clean microscope slide. Add one drop of *methylene blue* (a suitable stain for *animal cells*) and one drop of glycerine.

4. Stir the cells, stain and glycerine together and leave for 30 seconds. (This time can be adjusted according to the depth of staining required.)

5. Carefully place a clean, dry cover slip over the preparation, and then wrap a filter paper around the slide and cover slip.

6. Place the slide on a bench and press firmly with your thumb on the filter paper over the cover slip. The filter paper should absorb any surplus stain and glycerine, and the slide is then ready for viewing with a microscope (medium to high power).

The following structures (Figure 1.2) should be visible:

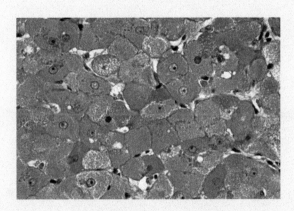

Figure 1.2(a) Stained liver cells

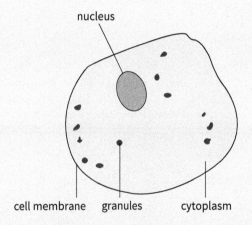

Figure 1.2(b) Animal cell (liver)

Aim: To observe plant cells

1. Peel off the dry outer leaves of an onion bulb.

2. Remove one of the fleshy leaves beneath.

3. Preferably using forceps, but fingers would do, peel away the outer skin-like covering (*epidermis*) of the fleshy leaf.

4. Place three drops of dilute *iodine solution* on a clean, dry microscope slide. (Iodine solution is a suitable temporary stain for *plant* cells.)

5. Transfer a small piece of the epidermis (a 50–75 mm square is large enough) to the iodine solution (make sure it lies flat and is completely covered by the iodine solution).

6. Carefully place a glass cover slip on top of the preparation, remove any excess liquid with a piece of filter paper and transfer the slide to the stage of a microscope.

The following structural features (Figure 1.3) should be visible (owing to the large size of the onion cells, it may not be necessary to use the high power of your microscope).

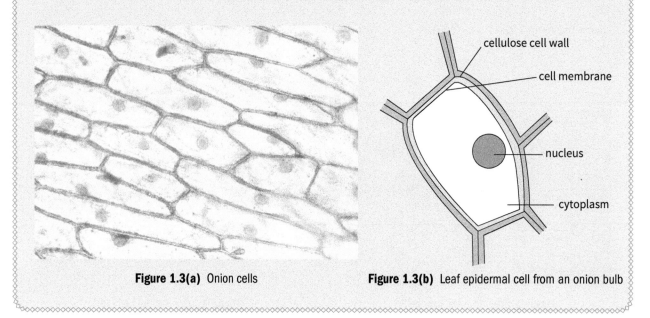

Figure 1.3(a) Onion cells   **Figure 1.3(b)** Leaf epidermal cell from an onion bulb

Specialised cells, tissues and organs

In unicellular organisms, one cell must be able to carry out *all* the functions of a living organism. In multicellular organisms, cells are usually modified to carry out *one* main function. The appearance of the cell will vary depending on what that main function is.

Thus, *there is a relationship between the structure and the particular function of a cell.*

Examples of this relationship are discussed here.

Root hair cell

Function
To absorb water and mineral ions (salts) from the soil.

How it is adapted to this function
The outer part of its cell wall (i.e. the part in direct contact with the soil) is in the form of a long, tubular extension (the ***root hair***, see Figure 1.4).

This root hair is

1. able to form a very close contact with the water film surrounding many soil particles, and

2. it greatly ***increases the surface area of the cell*** (Figure 1.4(b)) available for uptake of water and ions (also for the uptake of ***oxygen*** necessary for the respiration of all the cells in the root).

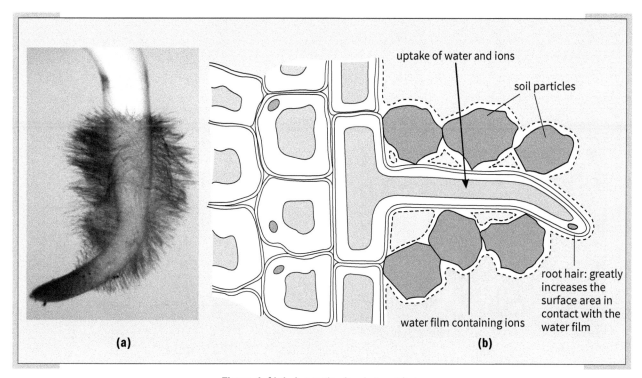

(a)

(b)

uptake of water and ions

soil particles

root hair: greatly increases the surface area in contact with the water film

water film containing ions

Figure 1.4(a) A root tip showing root hairs
(b) A root hair cell

Xylem vessels

Functions

1. *To conduct water and ions (dissolved salts)* **from the roots to the stem, leaves, flowers and fruits.**

2. *To provide support* **for the aerial parts of the plant.**

How they are adapted to these functions

Conduction
Xylem vessels are long narrow tubes (see figure 1.5), stretching from the roots, via the stem, to the leaves. They are stacked end to end like drain pipes.

Support
1. Their walls have been strengthened by the addition of the chemical **lignin**. (As the lignin in the walls builds up, it eventually kills the xylem vessels. There is then no layer of cytoplasm to restrict the flow of water and dissolved salts.)

2. Xylem vessels are part of the **vascular bundles**, which run through the stems of plants like iron reinforcements in concrete pillars – thus resisting bending strains caused by the wind.

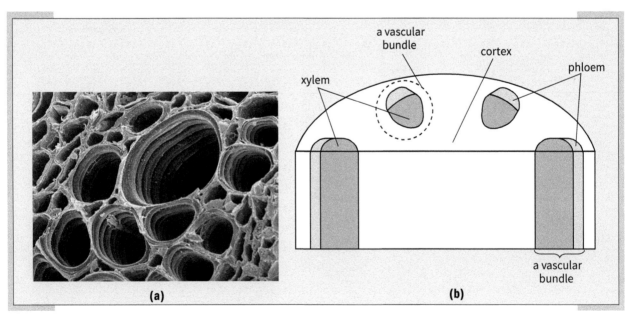

(a)   **(b)**

Figure 1.5(a) Xylem tissue in a plant stem
      (b) A section through a stem cut to show the arrangement of tissues in vascular bundles

Red blood cells

Function

To carry oxygen around the body.

How they are adapted to this function

1. Their cytoplasm contains the pigment **haemoglobin**, which combines (in the lungs) with oxygen to become oxyhaemoglobin.

2. They are **small** (7 μm × 2 μm) (and there are **many** of them) thus giving them a **very large surface area** for oxygen absorption (Figure 1.6).

3. They have a **bi-concave** shape, increasing their surface area for absorption still further.

4. They are flexible, allowing them to be pushed more easily through capillaries.

NOTE

Iron is a necessary component of the pigment haemoglobin.

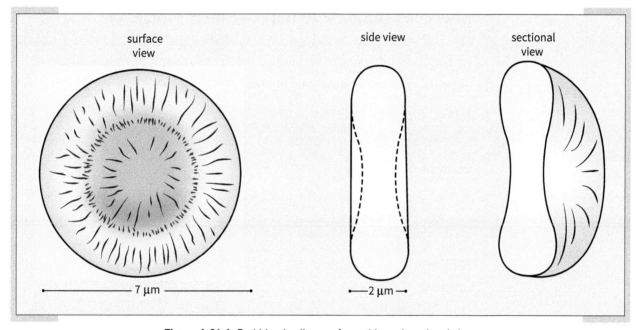

Figure 1.6(a) Red blood cells – surface, side and sectional views

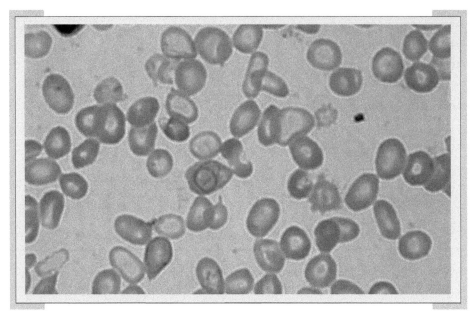

Figure 1.6(b) Photomicrograph of red blood cells

How cells combine to improve their efficiency

One cell working on its own would achieve very little in an individual plant or animal. Thus it is usual to find many similar cells lying side by side and working together, performing the same function.

Many similar cells working together and performing the same function are called a tissue.

Examples of tissues

* xylem tissue in the vascular bundles of a plant

* muscular tissue in the intestine wall of an animal

Different types of tissue often work together in order to achieve a combined function.

Several tissues working together to produce a particular function form an organ.

Examples of organs

* the leaf of a plant – an organ for the manufacture of carbohydrates during photosynthesis

* the eye of an animal – the organ of sight

Several different organs may be necessary in order to carry out a particular function.

A collection of different organs working together in order to perform a particular function is called an **organ system**.

Examples of organ systems

* the sepals, petals, stamens and carpels (i.e. the flowers) of a plant – for reproduction

* the heart, arteries, veins and capillaries in an animal, i.e. the circulatory system

An **organism** is *a collection of organ systems working together.*

The increasing order of cell organisation found within any living organism is thus

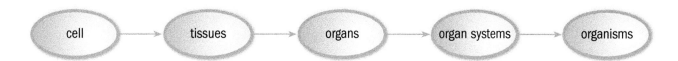

 Movement in and out of cells

Diffusion and osmosis

For plants and animals to stay alive, chemicals must be able to move easily:

* from one part of a cell to another

* into and out of a cell

* from one cell to another.

It is an advantage if this movement requires no effort (or, more correctly, no expenditure of energy) on the part of the organism, and, so long as there is no obstruction, chemical molecules carry out this process by **diffusion**.

Before diffusion can occur, there must be a **concentration gradient** of the molecules, i.e. a region of their (relatively) high concentration immediately beside a region of their (relatively) low concentration.

Diffusion can then be defined as *the movement of molecules from a region of their higher concentration to a region of their lower concentration, down a concentration gradient.*

Examples of diffusion

1. In plants:
    *   the movement of **carbon dioxide** into leaves during photosynthesis. Carbon dioxide in solution moves **from the water film** surrounding the mesophyll cells inside a leaf **to the chloroplasts** in the mesophyll cells.

    *   the movement of **water vapour** from the water film surrounding the mesophyll cells inside a leaf **through the intercellular spaces** of the leaf and **out through the stomata** (during **transpiration**).

2. In animals:
    *   the movement of **oxygen** after it has dissolved in the moisture lining the air sacs of the lungs **through the walls** of the air sacs (alveoli) into the blood.

    *   the movement of **carbon dioxide**, in solution, **from the cells** through tissue fluid **into the blood** in blood capillaries.

Understanding the processes of diffusion and osmosis

The movement of molecules by diffusion

Suppose a container is divided into two sections using a piece of cloth (Figure 1.7). A **dilute** sugar solution, which contains a lot of water, is poured into one side of the container. A concentrated sugar solution, which contains less water, is poured into the other side. The container is left to stand for a few minutes.

When checked, the concentration of the solution has changed on both sides of the container. Each side now has the **same** concentration of water and sugar.

By **diffusion**, both the water molecules and the sugar molecules would move down their respective concentration gradients, i.e. from high concentration to low concentration, until both sides were at the same concentration. The pores in the cloth would form no obstruction to the movement of the molecules in either direction.

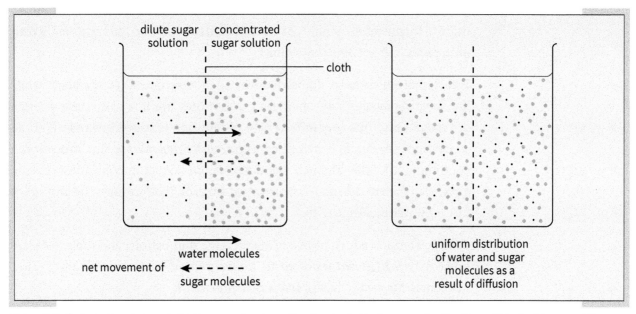

Figure 1.7 Sugar molecules moving one way and water molecules moving in the opposite direction until both sides are at the same concentration

The movement of molecules by osmosis

A similar experiment is carried out, but this time instead of the piece of cloth, the two sides of the container are separated using a ***membrane*** with microscopic holes in it (Figure 1.8). The holes are so small that they allow the passage of water molecules but ***not*** the sugar molecules. The same ***dilute*** sugar solution is poured into one side, and the same ***concentrated*** sugar solution is poured into the other. Again the container is left to stand for a few minutes.

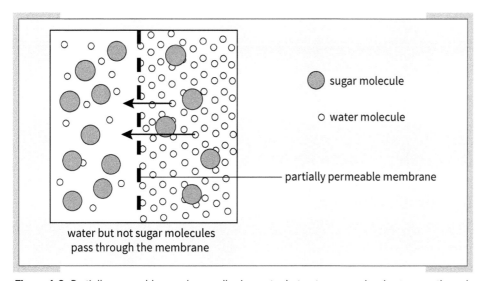

Figure 1.8 Partially permeable membrane allowing water but not sugar molecules to pass through

When checked, the **dilute** solution has **lost water molecules**, thus becoming more concentrated, while the **concentrated** solution has **gained water molecules** and become more dilute.

Water molecules have diffused down their concentration gradient, while the sugar molecules stay where they are as they are unable to pass through the membrane. This **specialised** case of diffusion is called **osmosis,** and the separating membrane is described as **partially permeable**. The process will continue until either the two solutions become equal in concentration or a force is applied to the more concentrated solution that prevents the passage of further water molecules.

Dilute solutions, which have a relatively large number of water molecules, are said to have a **high water potential. Concentrated** solutions, with fewer water molecules, are said to have a **low water potential**.

Osmosis can then be defined as *the passage of water molecules from a region of higher water potential to a region of lower water potential, through a partially permeable membrane.*

☑ *Try leaving a sugary sweet between your teeth and your cheek for 5 to 10 minutes, then remove it. You should be able to feel with your tongue that your cheek has become wrinkled in that area. Can you explain why this is so?*

☑ *Leave a few dried raisins (or currants) in a container of water overnight. The following day, see what has happened. Can you explain the result?*

How water is taken up by a plant

By simple diffusion
The cell wall of a root hair cell is made of cellulose, which is a **completely permeable** substance. Thus, the cell wall does not obstruct the passage of water into the root hair cell. Where the walls of neighbouring cells touch, water can pass into the root by simple **diffusion through** the cellulose of the cell walls (known as the **cell wall pathway**).

By osmosis

All cell membranes are ***partially permeable***. The cell sap of root hair cells has a relatively ***low*** water potential. Soil water has a relatively ***high*** water potential. Thus water will move into the vacuole of root hair cells by ***osmosis*** (known as the ***vacuolar pathway***) as shown in Figure 1.9.

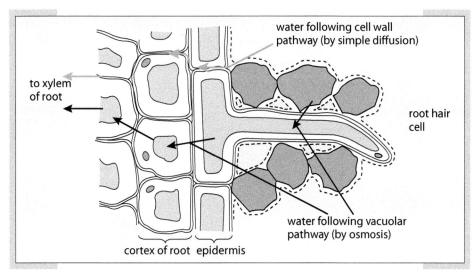

Figure 1.9 Uptake of water by osmosis (vacuolar pathway) and by diffusion (cell wall pathway)

Once water molecules have entered the root hair cell, their presence ***increases*** the water potential of that cell, compared with the next cell that is closer to the centre of the root. ***Osmosis*** will thus cause water to move into that cell from the root hair cell. This process continues until water molecules reach the ***xylem*** vessels in the centre of the root, and are then transported away to the stem. The effect of osmosis in the roots on water passage to the stem and leaves can be demonstrated as shown in Figure 1.10.

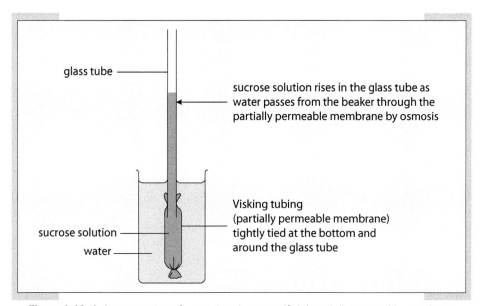

Figure 1.10 A demonstration of osmosis using an artificial partially permeable membrane

The effect of osmosis on plant and animal cells and tissues

The intake of water by osmosis

Water will always tend to enter **plant** (root) cells by osmosis, because the water potential of soil water is usually higher than the water potential of the plant's cell sap. As the vacuole thus increases in volume, it increasingly presses the cytoplasmic lining of the cell against the flexible, box-like cell wall (Figure 1.11). This pressure is called **turgor** pressure, and it helps to make plant cells firm.

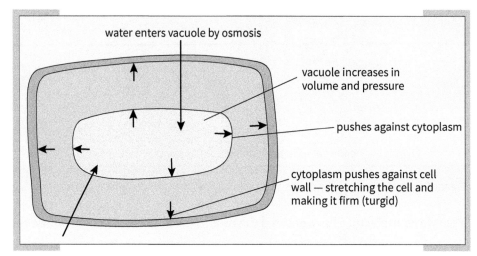

water enters vacuole by osmosis

vacuole increases in volume and pressure

pushes against cytoplasm

cytoplasm pushes against cell wall — stretching the cell and making it firm (turgid)

Figure 1.11 Plant cell in water

Turgor resulting from osmosis can be demonstrated using a tightly tied bag made of Visking tube (an artificial partially permeable membrane), filled with sugar solution, and placed in water for 20 minutes (Figure 1.12 (a)).

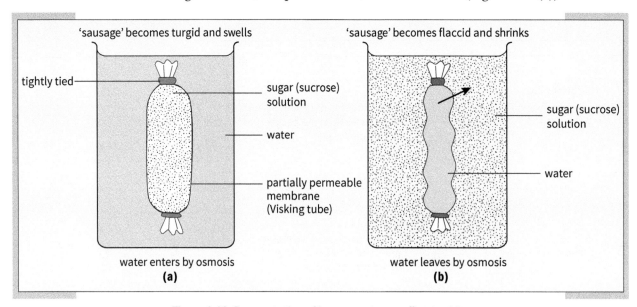

'sausage' becomes turgid and swells

'sausage' becomes flaccid and shrinks

tightly tied

sugar (sucrose) solution

water

partially permeable membrane (Visking tube)

sugar (sucrose) solution

water

water enters by osmosis
(a)

water leaves by osmosis
(b)

Figure 1.12 Demonstration of how osmosis can affect turgidity

Turgor in plant cells helps:

1. to keep ***stems upright***, and

2. to keep ***leaves flat*** so they can better absorb sunlight.

The water potential inside most ***animal*** cells is often the same as the solution in which the cells are naturally bathed. Thus there is little movement of water by osmosis into or out of the cell.

See The kidneys, later.

However, if a red blood cell is placed in a solution with a relatively high water potential, it starts to take in water by osmosis, and since there is ***no*** cell wall to resist the increased pressure that results, the cell ***bursts***.

The loss of water by (ex)osmosis

(When water leaves a cell by osmosis, the process is often called **exosmosis**.)

Plant cells placed in a solution of relatively low water potential lose water from their vacuoles. Since the cytoplasm is no longer being forced against the cell wall, they lose their turgor. They are said to become ***flaccid*** (Figure 1.13 (a)). Further exposure to a bathing solution of lower water potential will draw so much water from the vacuole that the cytoplasm is pulled away from the cell wall. Such a condition is called ***plasmolysis*** (Figure 1.13 (b)).

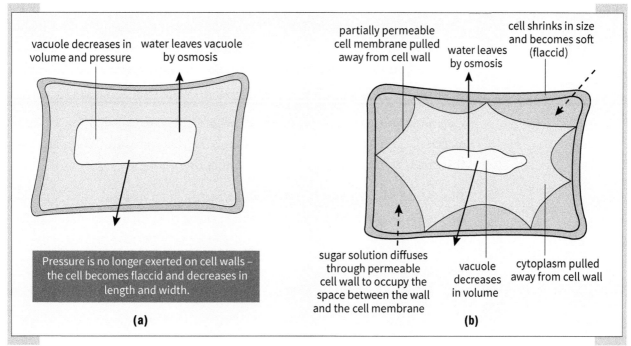

Figure 1.13(a) Plant cell in concentrated sugar solution (flaccid)
  (b) Plant cell in concentrated sugar solution (plasmolysed)

Animal cells placed in solutions of lower water potential, lose their shape and what turgidity they have, as water moves out of their cytoplasm. A red blood cell shrinks in size and its cell membrane becomes unevenly creased (crenated) as shown in Figure 1.14.

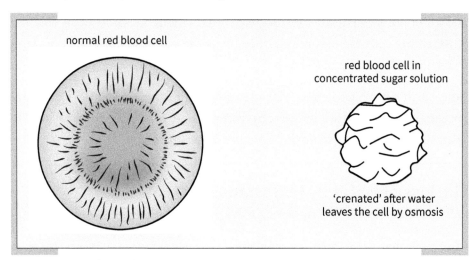

Figure 1.14 The effect of placing a red blood cell in a concentrated sugar solution

Figure 1.12(b) shows a demonstration of this effect using a Visking tubing 'sausage' containing a concentrated sugar solution when it is placed in a container of water and left for 20 minutes.

Active transport

Both plant and animal cells require a range of chemical molecules, other than water, for their metabolism, but these molecules may already be in a higher concentration inside the cell than outside it. Under such circumstances, a process of uptake is employed which requires the **expenditure** of considerable amounts of **energy**. This process is called **active transport**.

This situation arises in **plant roots**, where the **ions** needed for a plant's metabolism may be in very short supply in the soil water. Ions are thus absorbed by root hair cells by active transport.

The situation also arises in the **small intestine** of an **animal**, when digested food (such as **glucose**) is absorbed by the cells of the **villi** by active transport.

Active transport is thus defined as *the movement of ions into or out of a cell, through the cell membrane from a region of their lower concentration to a region of their higher concentration, against a concentration gradient, using energy released during respiration.*

The energy required is provided by the chemical reaction of **respiration** occurring in all living cells. Energy not immediately used in a cell is stored in a molecule called ATP, which then supplies the energy for active transport.

 **Enzymes**

An **enzyme** may be defined as *a protein that functions as a biological catalyst.*

Catalysts are particular chemicals that can affect ***how quickly*** chemical reactions occur. Only ***very small amounts*** of catalysts are needed to do their job. They are not used up or changed by the reactions they affect, which means that they can go on working, continuously catalysing the same reaction, so long as the reactant molecules (the ***substrate*** molecules) are present.

A catalyst is *a substance that speeds up a chemical reaction and is not changed by the reaction.*

Within cells, the chemical reactions occurring in the cytoplasm are also under the control of catalysts – ***biological*** catalysts – correctly called ***enzymes***.

Special properties of enzymes

1. They are all ***protein*** molecules.

2. They are made in the cytoplasm under instruction from genes on the chromosomes in the nucleus.

3. There is one particular ***temperature*** at which each enzyme works at its fastest rate. This is known as its ***optimum*** temperature, and for most enzymes in a mammal's body, this is around 37°C. As the temperature slowly approaches the optimum, the rate of enzyme activity gradually speeds up. Above the optimum, the rate of activity begins to slow down, until, at around 60°C, the enzyme is ***destroyed*** or ***denatured*** (not killed – it was never alive). Thus, the rate of the reaction falls to 0 (Figure 1.15).

 NOTE

Egg albumen is a protein. When it is heated, the protein is denatured, and remains permanently denatured (i.e. white) even when the egg cools down.

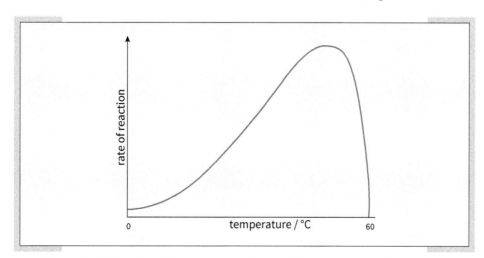

Figure 1.15 The effect of temperature on the rate of an enzyme-controlled reaction

NOTE

pH is a measure of the degree of acidity or alkalinity. A pH of 7 is neutral, below 7 is acidic and above 7 is alkaline.

4. There is one particular pH at which each enzyme works at its fastest rate. This is known as the *optimum pH*. For most enzymes in a mammal's body, this is around pH 7 (or slightly above), though for the enzyme *protease* in the *stomach*, its *optimum pH* is around **1.5** – created by the presence of stomach *hydrochloric acid*. Either side of the optimum pH, the rate of enzyme activity gradually decreases (Figure 1.16).

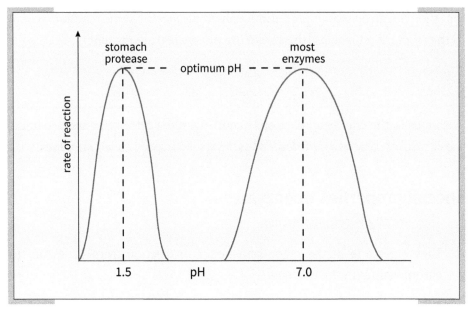

Figure 1.16 The effect of pH on the rate of an enzyme-controlled reaction

Aim:	To show the effect of temperature on enzyme action
Apparatus:	• water bath at 90°C (or beaker of boiling water + method of heating)
	• a refrigerator or bath of iced water
	• 3 test-tubes, each with a pipette
	• 3 beakers to support test-tubes
	• white spotting (or dimple) tile
	• 2 × 5 cm³ syringes
	• starch solution (0.5%)
	• amylase solution (0.5%)
	• iodine solution
	• timer

Method:
- In each of the test-tubes, use a syringe to add 1 cm³ amylase solution. Place test-tube 1 in the hot water, test-tube 2 in the refrigerator or iced water, and leave test-tube 3 at room temperature and leave the test-tubes for 10 minutes.
- In three rows, labelled 1, 2 and 3, place at least 10 separate, single drops of iodine solution.
- Keeping the test-tubes in their respective places, use the second syringe to add 1 cm³ starch solution to each test-tube and shake the tubes to mix.
- After 30 seconds, using the separate pipettes, add one drop of each mixture to the first drop of iodine solution in the appropriate row on the tile. In a table, record the colour after each drop is added. Continue this procedure every 30 seconds until a drop from one test-tube no longer produces a blue/black colour. Remove the other two test-tubes from water bath and the refrigerator. Now keep both of them at room temperature and continue testing them every minute for starch.

Results: The first drops from each test-tube should turn blue/black, indicating the presence of starch. After a few minutes, a drop from test-tube 3 (at room temperature) should not turn blue/black, while drops from test-tubes 1 and 2 will continue to do so. Eventually, a drop from test-tube 2 (that was in the refrigerator) should not turn iodine blue/black.

Conclusion: The amylase in test-tube one has been destroyed by the high temperature, and has not digested the starch. The activity of the enzyme in test-tube 2 has been reduced by the low temperature, but low temperature has not destroyed the enzyme as it is still capable of digesting the starch. The enzyme has worked most quickly at room temperature.

Aim: **To show the effect of pH on enzyme action**

Apparatus:
- 3 test-tubes, each with a pipette
- test-tube rack or a beaker to support test-tubes
- white spotting (or dimple) tile
- 2 × 5 cm³ syringes
- starch solution (0.5%)
- amylase solution (0.5%)
- iodine solution
- bench dilute hydrochloric acid + pipette
- bench dilute sodium hydroxide + pipette

Method:	• In three rows, labelled 1, 2 and 3, place at least 10 separate, single drops of iodine solution.
	• Place five drops of dilute hydrochloric acid in test-tube 1, five drops of dilute sodium hydroxide (an alkali) in test-tube 2, and five drops of distilled water in test-tube 3. Add 1 cm³ amylase and 1 cm³ starch solution to each tube, shake to mix and leave in the test-tube rack at room temperature.
	• After 30 seconds, using the separate pipettes, add one drop of each mixture to the first drop of iodine solution in the appropriate row on the tile. In a table, record the colour after each drop is added. Continue thus procedure every 30 seconds until a drop from one test-tube no longer produces a blue/black colour.
Results:	The first drops from each test-tube should turn blue/black, indicating the presence of starch. After a few minutes, a drop from test-tube 3 (neutral pH) should not turn blue/black, while drops from test-tubes 1 (acidic) and 2 (alkaline) will continue to do so.
Conclusion:	The amylase works best at a pH in the region of 7 (neutral), while a pH of below 7 (acidic) and above 7 (alkaline) prevents the enzyme from working. (This could be supported by further tests over a period of several minutes.)

NOTE

A hypothesis is a proposed explanation for a process. Further research is necessary before it can be confirmed.

How enzymes work – the 'lock and key' hypothesis

The job of an enzyme (e.g., those used in digestion) is often to break down a large molecule (the **substrate** molecule) into smaller molecules (the **product**). The 'lock and key' hypothesis suggests how this may be achieved.

Each enzyme is a molecule with a **specific shape**. On part of its surface is the **active site** (the **'lock'**) – a section into which its substrate molecule (the **'key'**) fits **exactly** (Figure 1.17). When the substrate molecule is in position in the active site, the enzyme then slightly stresses (or 'bends') the substrate, splitting it into two product molecules which drift away from the enzyme molecule leaving its active site free to operate again. Often by including a molecule of water in this process, the newly exposed ends of the product molecules are 'sealed' so that they will not re-join. This type of enzyme-controlled reaction, common in digestion, is known as **hydrolysis**.

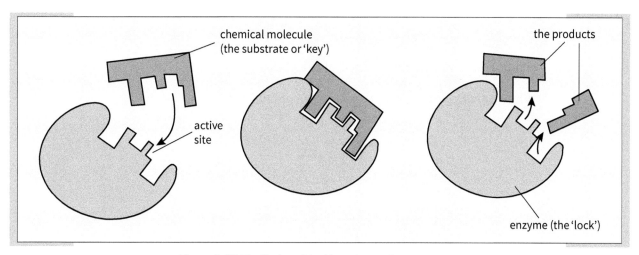

Figure 1.17 The 'lock and key' hypothesis of enzyme action

The 'lock and key' hypothesis explains enzyme action because:

1. Only the correct enzyme–substrate combination can work.

2. Increased temperature increases the rates at which the molecules of enzyme and substrate move, thus increasing the rate with which substrate molecules enter and product molecules leave the active site of the enzyme.

3. Extreme heat causes the atoms of the enzyme molecule to move so violently that they change position relative to one another – thus changing the shape of the active site so the enzyme stops doing its job.

4. Changes in pH are known to alter the shape of large molecules like proteins. When that protein is an enzyme, and as the shape of the active site changes, the enzyme will work less efficiently.

Points to remember

* Know the similarities and differences between plant and animal cells.

* Know the difference between ***tissue, organ*** and ***organ system*** and be able to define each.

* Be able to define ***diffusion*** and ***osmosis***.

* Learn what is meant by ***active transport***.

* Be able to write down definitions of the following terms: ***plasmolysis, turgor, water potential, partially permeable membrane***.

Exam-style questions for you to try

1. Figure 1.18 shows a cell from the leaf of a plant.

   Which labelled feature is also found in an animal cell?

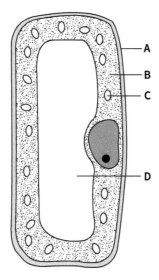

Figure 1.18

2. In what way are red blood cells adapted to carry oxygen?

   A. They have a nucleus containing haemoglobin.

   B. They have an increased surface area.

   C. They contain lignin which absorbs oxygen.

   D. They have strengthened cell walls.

3. The following are structures found in living organisms:

   P. the eye

   Q. the muscles in the intestine wall

   R. a flower

   Which shows the level of organisation in these three structures?

	tissue	organ	organ system
A	P	Q	R
B	Q	R	P
C	R	P	Q
D	Q	P	R

4. Figure 1.19 shows two liquids separated by a partially permeable membrane at the start of an experiment.

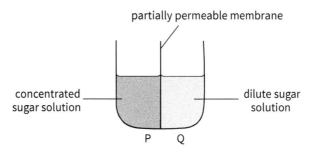

Figure 1.19

Which shows and explains the results 20 minutes later?

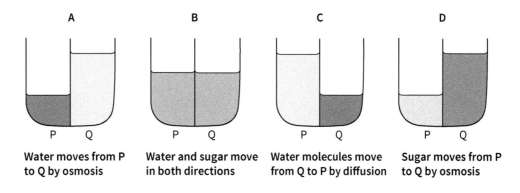

A	B	C	D
Water moves from P to Q by osmosis	**Water and sugar move in both directions**	**Water molecules move from Q to P by diffusion**	**Sugar moves from P to Q by osmosis**

5. Figure 1.20 shows the rate of an enzyme-controlled chemical reaction taking place in a test-tube that is gradually heated from 0°C to 60°C.

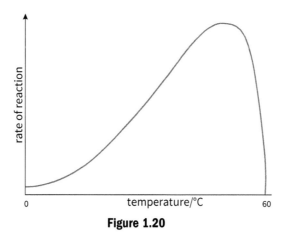

Figure 1.20

Which shows how the rate of reaction would change as the test-tube is then gradually cooled from 60°C back to 0°C?

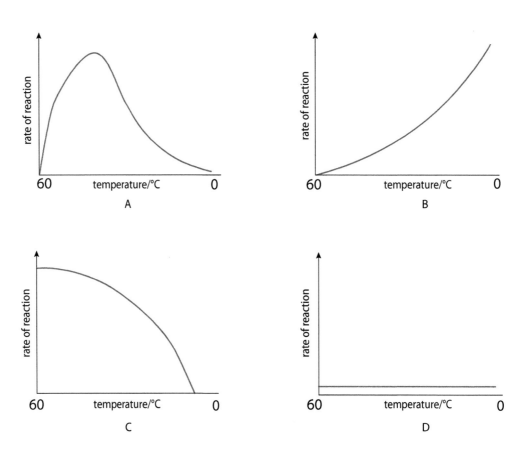

6. A student was asked to make a model of a plant cell. She took a length of tubing made from a substance that allows only water molecules to pass through and enclosed it in a flexible permeable membrane as shown in Figure 1.21.

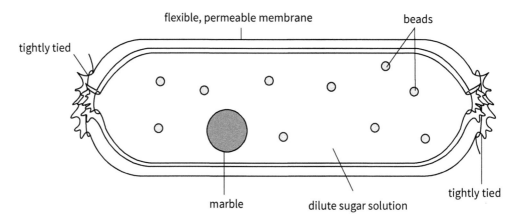

Figure 1.21

(a) Name the structures found in a plant mesophyll cell that are best represented by the following items used in her model:

the marble ....

the beads ....

the tubing .... [3]

(b) State a structure found in a plant cell that is **not** represented in the student's model.

.... [1]

(c) The student then placed her model into concentrated sugar solution for half an hour.

State and explain the similarities between what might happen to her model during that time and what would happen to a plant cell placed in the same solution.

....

....

....

....

....

....

....

....

.... [6]

Cambridge O Level Biology 5090 Paper 22 Q1 November 2011

7. With reference to a human being, explain

(a) what is meant by a *cell*

....

....

....

.... [3]

(b) how tissues and organs work together in the circulatory system.

....

....

....

....

....

....

....

....

.... [7]

Cambridge O Level Biology 5090 Paper 21 Q8 November 2010

You may need to look at
Chapter 3 to help you a
little with part b.

2 Nutrition

This chapter starts with an account of nutrition in plants, and explains in detail the laboratory experiments associated with photosynthesis. There follows a description of human diet and how to test for its major components. It concludes with an account of the alimentary canal and how it is involved in the processing of food.

Nutrition is one of the characteristics of living organisms. Every organism takes in, or makes, food which it uses for its survival.

 Plant nutrition

From the Greek:
'auto' = self
'trophic'= feeding

Green plants are described as autotrophic. They use small molecules readily available around them (***carbon dioxide*** from the ***air*** and ***water*** from the ***soil***) and build them up into ***large organic molecules*** (of the carbohydrate ***glucose***) during the chemical reaction known as ***photosynthesis***. The glucose that is made is then usually turned to ***starch*** and stored.

Photosynthesis

The linking together of carbon dioxide and water molecules requires energy. This is provided by sunlight which is trapped by the green, magnesium-containing chemical called ***chlorophyll*** found within the ***chloroplasts***, which is the site of photosynthesis inside a cell.

It is possible to show, experimentally, that carbon dioxide, light energy and chlorophyll are necessary for the process of photosynthesis, using potted plants (e.g., *Pelargonium* – a member of the *Geraniaceae* family). It is difficult to show that water is necessary for photosynthesis, since the removal of water from a plant may have serious effects other than on photosynthesis.

Aim:	**To show that carbon dioxide is necessary for photosynthesis**
Apparatus: (shown in Figure 2.1)	• two well-watered de-starched potted plants (e.g., *Pelargonium* or *Coleus*) • two polythene bags that will fit over the pots • cotton (to tie the polythene bag over the pot and around the stem) • a large piece of flat glass, two bell jars, some petroleum jelly • a small beaker containing concentrated sodium hydroxide (follow all the safety precautions when handling)
For destarching the plants:	Before the experiment, the plants should be kept in a dark place (e.g., a cupboard) for 24–48 hours, so that any starch present in their leaves has been used up. It is important because these types of plants immediately turn any glucose they make into starch and we will be testing the leaves after the experiment to see if any starch is present. You must therefore make sure that no starch is present before you begin the experiment.
Method: (shown in Figure 2.1)	Set up as follows: The two plants are left side by side in sunlight for about 8 hours, after which a leaf is taken from each plant and tested for the presence of starch.

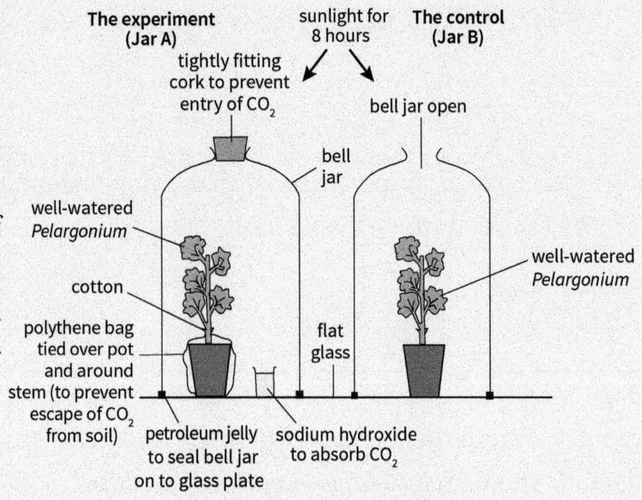

The experiment (Jar A) — sunlight for 8 hours — The control (Jar B)

tightly fitting cork to prevent entry of CO$_2$

bell jar open

bell jar

well-watered *Pelargonium*

cotton

polythene bag tied over pot and around stem (to prevent escape of CO$_2$ from soil)

petroleum jelly to seal bell jar on to glass plate

sodium hydroxide to absorb CO$_2$

flat glass

well-watered *Pelargonium*

Figure 2.1 Experiment to show carbon dioxide is necessary for photosynthesis

The starch test for a leaf:	1. Transfer the leaf to a beaker of **boiling** water for about 1 minute. 2. If a Bunsen burner is used to boil the water, **it must now be turned off**. 3. Transfer the leaf to a large test-tube which is half-full of methylated spirits (meths). 4. Place the test-tube (with the leaf in the meths) into the recently boiled water, and allow the heat of the water to bring the meths to the boil. As it does so, the chlorophyll is removed from the leaf, but the leaf becomes brittle. 5. Remove the leaf from the meths, and rinse it in the hot water. This will soften the leaf. 6. Spread the leaf on a white tile and add **iodine solution**. 7. If starch is present, the leaf will turn **blue/black** – if not, it will **stain brown**.
Results:	Leaf from Jar A stains brown. There is no starch present. Leaf from Jar B stains blue/black. Starch is present.
Conclusion:	Since only Jar B contained carbon dioxide, but, otherwise, conditions in the two jars were identical, carbon dioxide is necessary for photosynthesis.

Aim:	**To show that light is necessary for photosynthesis**
Apparatus:	• a well-watered, de-starched, potted plant (e.g., *Pelargonium* or *Coleus*)
	• a cork cut into two pieces
	• a pin

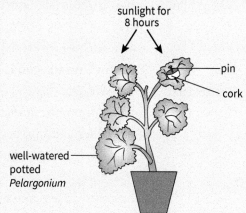

Method: The apparatus is set up as shown in Figure 2.2. The cork is fixed in the evening so that the leaf has time to destarch over night.

The experiment is left in sunlight for 8 hours. The cork is removed from the leaf, and the starch test is carried out on the leaf.

Results: Where the cork covered the leaf, the leaf stained **brown**. The rest of the leaf stained **blue/black**.

Figure 2.2 Experiment to show that light is necessary for photosynthesis

Conclusion: Only where light had been able to reach the leaf had starch been made; thus, light is necessary for photosynthesis.

Aim: **To show that chlorophyll is necessary for photosynthesis**

Apparatus: • a well-watered, de-starched, **variegated**, potted plant (e.g., *Pelargonium* or *Coleus*)

Note: A variegated plant has leaves which are green where chlorophyll is present, and white (usually) where there is no chlorophyll.

Method: Leave the plant in sunlight for 8 hours, after which remove one leaf and carry out the starch test on it.

Results: (See Figure 2.3.) The white area stains **brown** (no starch present); the green area stains **blue/black** (starch present).

Before starch test

white (no chlorophyll)

green (containing chlorophyll)

After starch test

brown (no starch present)

blue/black (starch present)

Figure 2.3 Experiment to show that chlorophyll is necessary for photosynthesis

Conclusion: Since starch has been made only where there was chlorophyll, chlorophyll is necessary for photosynthesis.

After carrying out the three experiments described above, it is possible to deduce that carbohydrate (starch) is produced when a plant has access to carbon dioxide, sunlight and chlorophyll.

There is, however, also a waste product of the process (oxygen), and this can be shown if a water plant is allowed to photosynthesise in the laboratory.

Aim: **To show that oxygen is given off during photosynthesis**

Apparatus:
- large beaker
- short-stemmed funnel
- two thick coins (to act as funnel supports)
- sodium hydrogencarbonate powder (to supply carbon dioxide to the plant)
- test-tube
- water weed, e.g., *Elodea* (Canadian pond weed) or *Hydrilla*

Method: Set up the apparatus as shown in Figure 2.4, and leave it over a 2-day period in a place where it will receive sunlight.

Results: A gas collects at the top of the test tube which is found to **relight** a **glowing splint**.

Conclusion: Only oxygen has the power to relight a glowing splint, and thus oxygen has been released during photosynthesis.

The control for this experiment is to place an exactly similar set-up in a dark cupboard for the same length of time. No gas collects in the test-tube.

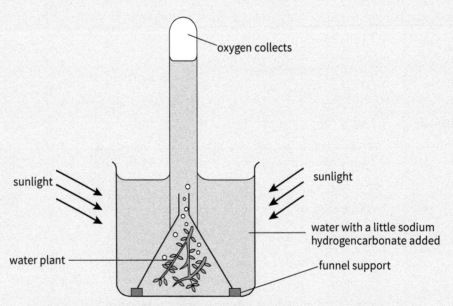

Figure 2.4 Experiment to show that oxygen is given off during photosynthesis

The release of oxygen by a water plant can be used to show what effect varying the individual requirements for photosynthesis has on the rate at which the process takes place.

The rate of photosynthesis

We can now look at a plant's **rate** of photosynthesis, that is, how quickly it photosynthesises. This rate changes if we vary the levels of the factors that are necessary for the process: light, carbon dioxide and temperature. The effect is shown by the amount of oxygen released by a water plant as it photosynthesises.

Aim: **To show the effect of varying light intensity on the rate of photosynthesis**

Apparatus: • short-stemmed funnel
                 • a large beaker
                 • a bench lamp
                 • a length of stem from a water-plant (e.g., *Elodea* or *Hydrilla*)
                 • a timer
                 • a test-tube and sodium hydrogencarbonate powder

Method: The apparatus is set up as shown in Figure 2.5.

Note: It is better to carry out the experiment in a darkened room so that the only source of light reaching the plant is the bench lamp.

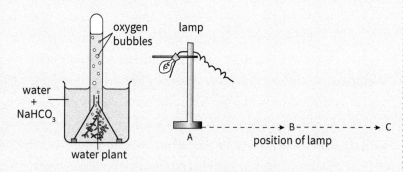

Figure 2.5 Experiment to show the effect of varying light intensity on photosynthesis

As the water plant photosynthesises, bubbles are released from the cut end of the stem. Place the bench lamp at position A. Leave the plant for about 10 minutes – this allows the plant time to adjust to the conditions), and then count the number of bubbles released by the plant for a measured period of time (e.g., 3 minutes). Move the lamp to position B. Again leave the plant for 10 minutes before counting the bubbles for the same measured period of time.

Move the lamp to position C, and repeat the procedure.

Results: As the lamp is moved further away, the intensity of light reaching the plant decreases. As the light intensity decreases, so does the number of bubbles released by the cut stem over the same period of time.

Conclusion: The rate of photosynthesis decreases with decreased light intensity.

Aim: **To show the effect of varying the carbon dioxide concentration on the rate of photosynthesis**

Apparatus:
- a large beaker
- a bench lamp and short-stemmed funnel
- a length of water-plant stem
- a timer
- sodium hydrogencarbonate powder

Method: When sodium hydrogencarbonate dissolves in water, it supplies the water with carbon dioxide.

$$NaHCO_3 \longrightarrow NaOH + CO_2$$

Immerse the length of stem in a test-tube filled with tap water. The water should be at room temperature. Leave it for about 20 minutes to adjust to the conditions. Place the bench lamp about 25 cm away and direct it at the plant. Count the number of bubbles released by the cut stem over a period of, say, 3 minutes and record the results.

Carefully weigh out 0.25 g of sodium hydrogencarbonate and add it to the water in the beaker. Gently stir the water to dissolve the powder, then leave for 20 minutes. Again place the bench lamp 25 cm away from the plant then count and record the number of bubbles released over 3 minutes.

Repeat process for two further additions of 0.25 g of hydrogencarbonate.

Results: More carbon dioxide becomes available to the plant as more sodium hydrogencarbonate is added. As more carbon dioxide becomes available, so the number of bubbles released by the cut stem in 3 minutes increases.

Conclusion: As the amount of carbon dioxide available to the plant increases, so does the amount of carbon dioxide released from it. The increased amounts of available carbon dioxide increase the rate of photosynthesis.

Aim: **To show the effect of varying the temperature on the rate of photosynthesis**

Apparatus:
- a large test-tube
- a bench lamp
- a length of water-plant stem (e.g., *Elodea* or *Hydrilla*)
- 2 beakers of different sizes
- a timer
- a thermometer and sodium hydrogencarbonate powder

Method: Set up the apparatus as in the two previous experiments, but this time, immersed in a larger beaker of water. This acts as a water bath, the temperature of which may be altered using ice or warm water (e.g., from a tap). Lower the temperature of the water bath by adding ice, then leave for 20 minutes to allow the stem to adjust to the conditions. Count the number of bubbles released by the cut stem over a period of 3 minutes and record the results. Raise the temperature of the water bath by adding warm water. Again give the plant time to adjust before counting the bubbles released. With only the temperature of the water being altered, and with the plant being left for 20–30 minutes at each new temperature to adjust to the conditions, the effect of varying temperature on the number of bubbles released by the cut stem is investigated.

Note: At temperatures above room temperature, the thermometer must be checked regularly while the plant is adjusting to the conditions, and the water bath topped up with warm water as necessary to maintain a steady temperature.

Results: The higher the temperature (up to around 45°C), the more bubbles are released per unit time.

Conclusion: The higher the temperature, up to about 45°C, the faster the rate of photosynthesis.

The importance of a control

In all of the above experiments, a comparison is made between a leaf (or part of a leaf) which was able to function with all the requirements for photosynthesis, and a leaf (or part of one) where one of the requirements is missing. In this way, the results of the experiment are shown to be **valid**.

The apparatus and materials which provide this comparison make up the **control** to the experiment. Wherever possible, **all** biological experiments should have a control.

 ✔ *When a new drug is being tested (or 'trialed') on a number of volunteers, can you suggest how a control can be built into the trial?*

 NOTE

When performing experiments, remember always to include a control in order to make your experiment valid, and repeat the experiments several times, taking an average of your results, in order to reduce experimental error to a minimum.

Experimental error and the need to repeat experiments

To reduce experimental error, each of the above experiments should, ideally, be repeated several times, and an average of the results taken.

 ✔ *For each of the experiments, or demonstrations, above, list the possible causes of experimental error.*

The concept of limiting factors

The availability of light, carbon dioxide, water and a suitable temperature all affect the rate of photosynthesis. However, the rate of photosynthesis in a plant at any time is governed by whichever one of these factors is in **shortest supply**, i.e. that factor will limit the rate of photosynthesis, even though all other factors may be ideal (or optimum). These are thus described as **limiting factors**.

How plants obtain the necessary raw materials and carry out the process of photosynthesis

See section on transpiration.

The intake of water

For the majority of plants, roots absorb the **water** necessary for photosynthesis **from the soil** (from where it has to be carried to the leaves).

Refer to Chapter 1.

A few millimetres behind the tip of every root, and extending also for a few millimetres, lies the **region of root hairs**. The very numerous root hair cells thus provide a **very large surface area** for the uptake of water (and of ions) from the soil. The earlier section on osmosis explains how water is absorbed by the root hair cells.

The intake of carbon dioxide

For the majority of plants, leaves:

* absorb the **carbon dioxide** from the **air**
* absorb sunlight energy
* manufacture carbohydrate
* release the waste product, oxygen.

NOTE

The number to remember here is '6'. Each chemical in the equation in symbols begins with a 6. There are six molecules of carbon dioxide, of water and of oxygen, and there are six atoms of carbon in the glucose.

The equation for photosynthesis

$$\text{carbon dioxide} + \text{water} \xrightarrow[\text{chlorophyll}]{\text{light energy}} \text{carbohydrate} + \text{oxygen}$$

$$6CO_2 + 6H_2O \xrightarrow[\text{chlorophyll}]{\text{light energy}} \underset{\text{(glucose)}}{C_6H_{12}O_6} + 6O_2$$

Sunlight provides the energy necessary to combine carbon dioxide and water molecules to form carbohydrate. That energy becomes 'locked away' within the carbohydrate molecule as **chemical energy**.

Photosynthesis is thus a process in which light energy is converted into chemical energy. If a living organism then dismantles (i.e. breaks down) the carbohydrate molecule (during a metabolic process – usually **respiration**), the energy is released.

Until the molecule is broken down, it is often stored. The first carbohydrate made during photosynthesis is glucose, but this is soluble, affecting concentration and thus enzyme action within a cell. It is therefore usually converted to the **insoluble** carbohydrate, **starch**. Starch is first stored in the **chloroplast** where it has just been made by the photosynthesising cell. It is then converted to **sucrose** to be carried to the storage organs of the plant (usually the root or stem). Here, sucrose is reconverted to starch. A (stem) **tuber** of the **potato** plant is an example of a plant storage organ that **stores starch**.

How plants obtain carbon dioxide from the air through their leaves

Most, and sometimes all, of a plant's photosynthesis takes place in the leaves. Leaves are **organs** containing several different **tissues** with cells adapted to perform their own particular roles as efficiently as possible.

Leaf structure

(The main features of which are shown in Figure 2.6)

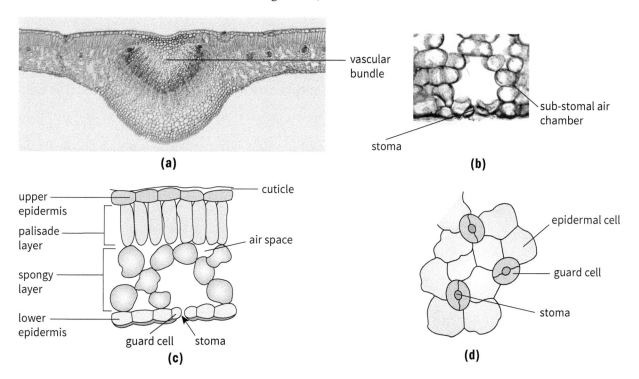

Figure 2.6(a) Transverse section of a dicotyledonous leaf: whole leaf showing the vascular bundle of the large central vein (the midrib)
  (b) Transverse section of a dicotyledenous leaf: stoma and sub-stomal air chamber
  (c) A leaf in transverse section to show a stoma
  (d) Stomata on the undersurface of a leaf

The structure of a leaf and how it is adapted for photosynthesis

Cuticle

A waxy non-cellular covering to the leaf. It

* is waterproof
* is transparent to allow light to enter
* provides some protection from mechanical forces.

Upper epidermis

A single layer of cells which

* secrete the cuticle
* have **no** chloroplasts thus allowing light to reach the cells beneath.

Palisade cells

One layer (or two, depending on species) of closely packed, elongated cells with a water film coating their walls. They

* are first to receive light
* have the greatest concentration of chloroplasts.

Chloroplasts

* contain chlorophyll for photosynthesis
* provide a large surface area for the uptake of carbon dioxide
* are where photosynthesis occurs in the cell
* usually convert glucose to starch and store it temporarily
* in dim light, may move nearer to the illuminated surface of the cell.

Spongy cells

Cells with fewer chloroplasts, they are loosely packed with many air (intercellular) spaces between them. Their walls are again coated with a water film. They

* carry out some photosynthesis
* allow gases to diffuse freely throughout the leaf.

Note: Palisade and spongy cells are the photosynthesising cells in the middle of a leaf. They are referred to as **mesophyll** cells.

Together, their walls provide an enormous surface area for **gaseous exchange** as they **absorb carbon dioxide** and **release oxygen** during photosynthesis.

The vein (vascular bundle)

The vein contains two types of tissue, the **xylem** and the **phloem**.

NOTE

Mesophyll means middle of the leaf in Greek.

The xylem

- *strengthens* the leaf helping to resist tearing
- *transports water and ions* to the leaf.

The phloem

- *transports dissolved sugar* (sucrose) mostly away from the leaf, as well as **amino acids** both from and to the leaf as required.

The lower epidermis

It may be coated with a thin waxy cuticle. It forms the lower protective boundary to the leaf. The cells do not contain chloroplasts **except** the **guard cells** (Figure 2.7), which are specialised epidermal cells. Guard cells occur in pairs, each pair controlling the opening and closing of the pore (**stoma**) between them. The function of a stoma (plural: stomata) is during gaseous exchange:

- to allow carbon dioxide to enter the leaf for photosynthesis
- to allow oxygen to leave the leaf during photosynthesis
- to allow some exchange of these gases, in the opposite direction in low light intensities when the plant is respiring faster than it is photosynthesising.

Note: Stomata also allow water vapour (which is a gas) to leave a leaf during transpiration. Guard cells control the stoma as a result of their degree of turgidity (see osmosis). The asterisk relates to the note.

 NOTE

*The guard cells become turgid, but the thicker inner wall does not stretch as much as the outer, thinner one.

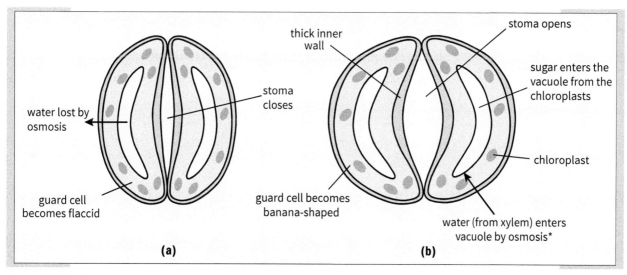

Figure 2.7(a) How guard cells control the size of a stoma in the dark
(b) How guard cells control the size of a stoma in the light

NOTE

It would be wise to collect several different types of leaf before you begin, since some work better than others.

✓ *Fold a leaf (e.g., Lantana) in half, so its upper surface comes into contact with itself, then tear the leaf along its fold. With practice, you should be able to leave a thin, transparent piece of lower epidermis along one side of the fold. Carefully remove this and transfer it to a drop of water on a microscope slide. Gently lower a cover slip onto the specimen, and using low power on your microscope, identify the guard cells. You may need a higher power to see the chloroplasts within the guard cells.*

✓ *To demonstrate the presence of stomata, submerge a leaf in a beaker of hot water, and watch as air bubbles form over the stomata as the air in the intercellular spaces expands and passes out of the leaf.*

How a leaf is involved in the process of photosynthesis

1. Carbon dioxide ***diffuses*** down a ***concentration gradient*** from the atmosphere through the ***stomata*** into a leaf.
2. Carbon dioxide ***diffuses*** freely throughout the leaf in the intercellular spaces.
3. Carbon dioxide ***dissolves*** in the film of water which surrounds the mesophyll cells and which has been delivered to the leaf in the xylem of the vascular bundles.
4. Carbon dioxide ***diffuses*** in solution into the mesophyll cells and passes to the chloroplasts where photosynthesis occurs.
5. Sugar made by photosynthesis is carried away (**translocated**) from the leaf in the phloem of the vascular bundles.
6. Oxygen diffuses from the mesophyll cells into the intercellular spaces and out through the stomata, across a concentration gradient into the atmosphere.

The importance of photosynthesis to the living universe

Photosynthesis produces the carbohydrate, with its chemical energy, upon which almost all other forms of life rely, though plants may convert this carbohydrate into protein or fat before it is passed on.

NOTE

See the carbon cycle.

The oxygen produced by photosynthesis is essential for the respiration of most life forms, and photosynthesis uses up the carbon dioxide released by respiration, converting it into carbohydrate.

Mineral nutrition in a plant

The importance of nitrogen-containing ions

Living organisms need **proteins** for growth and repair. Plants have to manufacture (synthesise) their own proteins and this they do by converting their carbohydrates first into amino acids and then linking the amino acids together to form proteins.

The additional element necessary to convert carbohydrate into amino acid is **nitrogen** and although the atmosphere is 79% nitrogen, plants cannot make direct use of it. The nitrogen used by a plant is absorbed from the soil as the **nitrate ion** (NO_3^-) via the root hairs.

The importance of magnesium ions

As with nitrates and all other ions, magnesium ions are also absorbed from the soil through the root hairs. Magnesium is the central atom in a chlorophyll molecule.

 **Animal nutrition**

Carbohydrates, fats and **proteins** are the three main classes of foods. Their chemical structures are described here.

Carbohydrates

These are organic chemicals containing the elements **carbon, hydrogen** and **oxygen** only. The ratio of atoms of hydrogen to atoms of oxygen in a carbohydrate molecule is always 2:1 (as in water – hence carbo**hydrate**).

Carbohydrates with large molecules such as **starch** and **glycogen** are insoluble (a starch 'solution' is in fact a starch suspension).

Smaller carbohydrate molecules are soluble, and occur as:

* **complex** sugars, such as **maltose** and **sucrose** (table sugar), all with the formula $C_{12}H_{22}O_{11}$, or
* **simple** sugars, such as **glucose** or **fructose**, with the formula $C_6H_{12}O_6$.

Fats (or oils if they are liquid at 20°C)

These, too, are organic chemicals which contain the elements **carbon, hydrogen** and **oxygen** only. This time, however, the ratio of H to O in the molecule is very much higher than 2:1. They are all **insoluble in water**, and are formed by the joining of a **glycerol** molecule with **fatty acid** molecules.

Proteins

These, again, contain the elements **carbon, hydrogen** and **oxygen**, but this time, **always nitrogen as well** (and often other elements such as sulphur and phosphorus).

They are large, usually insoluble molecules which are built up from simple, soluble units known as **amino acids**. Figure 2.8 shows how amino acids link together.

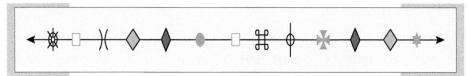

Figure 2.8 Amino acids linking to form a protein molecule
(each different symbol represents one of the 22 different amino acids)

Up to 100 amino acids linked together (by chemical bonds called **peptide** bonds) form a **polypeptide** – many more amino acids linked together form a protein.

Tests to show the presence of carbohydrates, fat and protein

Carbohydrates

	chemical (reagent) used	how test is carried out	result
starch	iodine solution	put a few drops on the substance to be tested	**blue/black** colour if starch is present (**brown** if starch is absent)
maltose and glucose	Benedict's solution	add a few drops to a solution of the substance to be tested and heat in a water bath at 90°C	**red, orange, yellow** or **green** if either of sugars is present (**blue** if not)

Note: Benedict's solution does not distinguish between the complex sugar 'maltose' and the simple sugar 'glucose'. In their reaction with Benedict's solution, both sugars work as chemicals known as 'reducing agents', and thus belong to a group of sugars referred to as **reducing sugars**, all of which react in this way.

Fats (the ethanol emulsion test)

reagent used	how test is carried out	result
ethanol	a dried* sample of the substance to be tested is mixed with ethanol which is then poured into a test tube of water	the water turns **cloudy** if fat is present but remains clear if it is not

Proteins (the biuret test)

reagent used	how test is carried out	result
biuret solutions 1 and 2	add equal volumes of solutions 1 and 2 to a solution of the substance to be tested	a **purple** colour indicates that protein is present a **blue** colour indicates that protein is absent

Biuret 1 contains sodium hydroxide, which is harmful to the skin, and thus appropriate safety precautions should be taken.

The three classes of food described above are three of seven important constituents of our diet. The seven are:

1. carbohydrates
2. fats
3. proteins
4. vitamins
5. mineral salts
6. fibre (or roughage)
7. water.

NOTE

*The test is more reliable if a dried sample is used, but if it is not possible to dry the sample, then the ethanol drained from it may already be cloudy, indicating the presence of a fat.

NOTE

Since 'biuret' is a chemical – not a person as in 'Benedict's solution', it does not begin with a capital letter – unless it is the first word in a sentence. Never say that a test is 'positive' or 'negative'. State the observed colour and the conclusion you draw from that result.

The principal sources of these seven constituents, and why they are important in our diets are shown in the table below.

constituent	source	importance
carbohydrate		
starch	potatoes beans and peas yams cassava cereals	carbohydrate molecules contain *energy* which is *released* in cells as the molecules are broken down during *respiration*
sugars	honey cane fruits	
fats		
	fat meat dairy foods egg yolk nuts avocado	fat molecules contain more *energy* than carbohydrates and are stored in the skin and around the kidneys
proteins		
	meat peas and beans fish egg white peanuts	proteins are used for *growth* and *repair* muscle is largely protein
vitamins		
C* (ascorbic acid)	citrus fruit (fresh) cabbage	for *healthy gums* and *skin repair*
D* (calciferol)	fish liver egg yolk the action of sun on the skin	for the *uptake of calcium* from the gut and for *strong tooth and bone* formation
mineral salts		
calcium*	flour milk	for *healthy bones* and teeth for *muscle action* and *blood clotting*
iron*	liver red meat spinach	for *haemoglobin* – the oxygen-carrying pigment in red blood cells

NOTE

*If any of these four constituents are lacking in the diet, then the person will suffer from a deficiency disease.

constituent	source	importance
fibre	fruit vegetables nuts	forms bulk in the intestines, giving muscles of peristalsis something to push against – *preventing constipation*
water	drinks all foods	*solvent* for chemicals in the body it is the medium for all chemical reactions. It is used to cool the body and makes up about 68% of body mass.

Plants manufacture their own food requirements; they are autotrophic. Animals obtain their nutritional requirements 'second-hand' by either eating plants or animals which have eaten plants (directly or indirectly), and are described as heterotrophic.

The constituents of an animal's diet are listed earlier in the chapter. However, for the animal to be healthy, its diet must contain these constituents in their correct amounts.

A diet which has the correct amount of each constituent is called a **balanced diet**.

Balanced diets differ depending on the lifestyle, age and sex of the person.

type of person	special requirements	reasons
child	protein carbohydrate calcium	for growth for energy for bones and teeth
active adult	carbohydrate protein	for *energy* and to *build muscles* if the job so requires
pregnant woman	iron salts calcium protein	for blood for baby's bones for making baby's cells

Note: The (basal) metabolic rate of males is higher than that of females, and thus, for a man and a woman both involved in identical activities, the man will require more energy from his diet. Fats provide the greatest amount of energy per unit mass – just over twice as much as carbohydrates and proteins. For this reason, eating a diet rich in fats is likely to lead to *obesity* (overweight), when the energy consumed exceeds the energy expended by the person.

NOTE

Fibre is made up largely of cellulose from the cell walls of plants. Cellulose is an insoluble carbohydrate.

Deficiency diseases that occur if certain constituents are lacking in the diet

Diet lacking in vitamin C

The person will develop bleeding gums and wounds do not heal properly. The disease is called **scurvy**.

Diet lacking in vitamin D

Growing bones become soft causing either bow legs or knock knees. The disease is called **rickets**. In older people, bones have a tendency to fracture.

Diet lacking in calcium

The skeleton does not form properly, with symptoms similar to those for lack of Vitamin D. Growth is stunted.

Diet lacking in iron

Insufficient haemoglobin is made for the carriage of oxygen. The person suffers from **anaemia**. They will be lacking in energy, and in severe cases, the deficiency leads to coma and death.

The problems of an unbalanced diet

A person's diet may be unsuitable for healthy growth for two main reasons:
1. The balance of constituents is incorrect – leading to malnutrition.
2. There is insufficient quantity – leading to starvation.

Malnutrition

Malnutrition has many effects of which constipation, heart disease and obesity are three of the more important.

1. **Constipation** is a result of **insufficient fibre** in the diet (see section on nutrients). Diet lacking in fibre may, over several years, lead to bowel cancer.
2. **Heart disease** can occur when animal fats and cholesterol* form **atheroma** on the walls of the **coronary artery** (carrying blood to the heart muscle). This restricts blood flow in the artery, decreasing oxygen supply to the heart muscle. In severe cases, the artery may become blocked, leading to a cardiac arrest ('heart attack'). The risk of heart

NOTE

*Cholesterol is a chemical that is classified, along with fats, as a **lipid**. Cholesterol is essential for normal health, e.g. for cell membrane production, but in excess can form deposits on artery walls.

disease is increased when blood pressure is high, and since atheroma decreases the bore of the arteries, it tends to increase blood pressure.

3. **Obesity** (overweight) is associated with high blood pressure and heart disease, since it is often the result of eating too much animal fat, and the heart has to work harder to move the increased bulk. It also may lead to: diabetes, stress on joints and social rejection.

Starvation

Starvation results in very restricted growth and development, particularly of muscles, leading to weakness. Resistance to disease is severely reduced, and death eventually follows.

Famine (a lack of adequate amounts of food to support the population) may result from

* poverty
* overpopulation
* drought
* flooding
* crop failure due to disease
* poor farming techniques
* war/political instability

or any combination of these.

The world as a whole produces sufficient food to sustain its current population, but some areas greatly overproduce, and the cost of transporting the food to where it is needed is too high for those requiring it. A 'world solution' needs to be sought.

Overpopulation may be overcome with education on, and availability of, birth control methods. Education may also help to improve farming techniques, and to help solve some of the problems of flooding, where poor farming techniques are to blame.

Biological research is developing disease-resistant crops and improved methods of disease control. An understanding of the effects of deforestation may go some way to improving the problems caused by both flooding and drought (see the section on the effects of humans on the ecosystem).

The human alimentary canal

Human (heterotrophic) nutrition involves **four** basic stages:

1. **Ingestion** – taking food into the digestive system – 'eating'.
2. **Digestion** – (i) mechanical – chopping and grinding food with teeth and muscular churning of the food as in the stomach.

   (ii) chemical – breaking large insoluble molecules into small, soluble ones (using enzymes).
3. **Absorption** – taking digested food into the bloodstream.
4. **Assimilation** – using the absorbed food in metabolic processes.

Any food which cannot be digested or absorbed is passed out of the alimentary canal during **egestion**. The main regions of the human alimentary canal are shown in Figure 2.9.

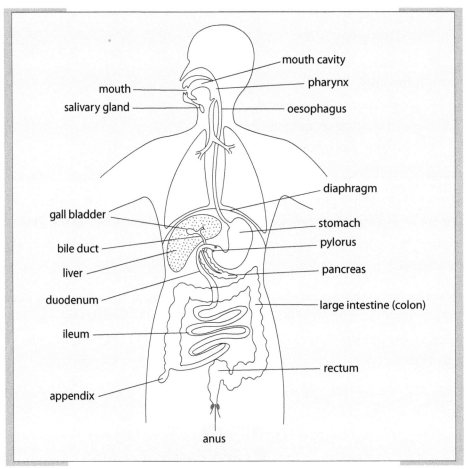

Figure 2.9 The human alimentary canal and associated organs

The functions of the main regions of the alimentary canal

The mouth

This is the opening through which food is ingested into the **buccal cavity** (or mouth cavity). The buccal cavity processes the food as follows:

* **Teeth** mechanically digest the food (see later).
* **Salivary glands** secrete a solution (saliva) of the enzyme **amylase** to digest starch and the protein *mucin*, which is sticky to bind the food together and to lubricate it.
* **The tongue** rolls the food into balls (boli – bolus in the singular) and pushes them to the back of the cavity for swallowing.

The oesophagus

This is a muscular tube down which waves of muscular contractions (**peristalsis**) pass, pushing each bolus towards the stomach as shown in Figure 2.10.

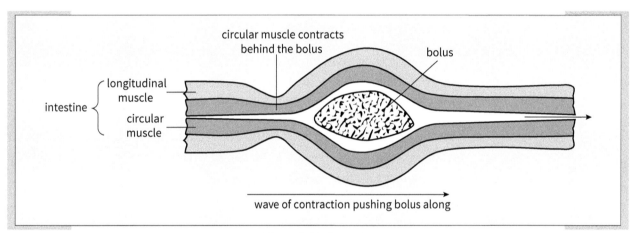

Figure 2.10 Peristalsis

The stomach

This is a muscular bag which churns the food for up to around 4 hours. Its wall secretes **gastric juice** which contains:

* the enzyme **protease** for starting the digestion of *proteins*, changing them to *polypeptides*
* *hydrochloric acid* to
  * provide the correct pH for protease to work
  * kill potentially harmful bacteria in food
* (in children only) the enzyme rennin to clot protein in milk.

> **NOTE**
>
> A sphincter is a ring of muscle that, in its contracted state, keeps a tube closed, allowing it to open when the muscle relaxes.

After treatment in the stomach, the food is in the form of soup-like 'chyme', which passes through a ring of muscle (the *pylorus* or pyloric *sphincter*) which relaxes to allow the food to enter the duodenum.

The duodenum

This is a tube about 30 cm long. It

1. receives *bile* via the bile duct from the liver
2. receives *pancreatic juice* via the pancreatic duct from the pancreas
3. releases a digestive juice from its walls (called intestinal juice) which contains *protease* and the enzyme *lipase* for fat digestion.

The pancreas

Lying between the stomach and the duodenum, this is an organ which secretes *pancreatic juice*, which it passes to the duodenum to help in digestion (as well as releasing the hormone insulin – see later).

Pancreatic juice contains the following enzymes:

1. *amylase* for digesting starch
2. *protease* for digesting protein
3. *lipase* for digesting fat.

The amylase completes the job started by the amylase in the buccal cavity, changing any remaining *starch* to *maltose* sugar.

The protease (now working in very slightly alkaline conditions, since alkaline bile from the liver neutralises the hydrochloric acid) changes any remaining *proteins* to *polypeptides*.

Fats are broken up into small droplets – emulsified – by the bile, greatly increasing their surface area. Lipase can now work on them far more quickly, changing *fats* into *fatty acids* and *glycerol*.

NOTE

The cork is to prevent the sodium hydroxide from coming into contact with your skin. If this does happen, rinse it off immediately with plenty of water under a tap.

Pour about 2 cm³ of water into a test-tube. Add about 0.5 cm³ of cooking oil. Place your thumb over the top of the test-tube and shake the tube vigorously for 5 seconds. Place the test-tube in a test-tube rack (or beaker). Repeat the procedure, but this time, preferably wearing rubber gloves, add about 0.25 cm³ of dilute sodium hydroxide, and put a tightly fitting cork into the test-tube before shaking it.

Compare the two test-tubes after about 5 minutes. The alkaline sodium hydroxide mimics the alkaline bile released onto fats by the liver. Can you explain what has happened to your cooking oil in the second tube?

The liver

The liver is the largest internal organ and is described as the 'chemical factory' of the body. Like the pancreas, it is not technically part of the alimentary canal, but its function of producing **bile** is closely associated with digestion. Bile is a greenish-coloured fluid. It is alkaline due to the salts it contains and is stored in the **gall bladder** before it is poured into the duodenum. Its functions are:

1. to neutralise acidic chyme from the stomach
2. to emulsify fat.

Large food molecules are almost ready for absorption, but first, enzymes in intestinal juice must change **maltose** to **glucose** (by the enzyme maltase) and **polypeptides** into **amino acids** (by another protease enzyme).

The ileum

This is the region where the **absorption** of digested food, and a good deal of the water, takes place. To improve its efficiency, its surface area is increased in the following ways:

1. It is about 7 m long (in a person).
2. Its walls are folded ('pleated') longitudinally.
3. Its walls have the appearance of velvet due to millions of microscopic finger-like projections called **villi**.

The colon

Its walls are folded (transversely, this time) to increase its surface area for **water absorption**. Infections of the colon lead to diarrhoea. Together with the rectum, it forms the large intestine.

Note: Food is moved steadily along the duodenum, ileum and colon by **peristalsis** (as in the oesophagus). The indigestible fibre forms the bulk against which the muscles of the intestines can push.

The rectum

This is a muscular storage chamber where the undigested food (faeces) is held and moulded before being pushed out through the anus during **egestion** (or defaecation).

The anus

This is the exit to the alimentary canal. It is closed by a ring of muscle (the anal sphincter), which is relaxed to allow egestion.

A summary of chemical digestion in the alimentary canal

name of food	where digested	enzyme involved	product
starch	buccal cavity	amylase	maltose
starch	duodenum	amylase (from pancreas)	maltose
maltose	duodenum	maltase	glucose
proteins	stomach	protease	polypeptides
proteins	duodenum	protease (from pancreas)	polypeptides
polypeptides	duodenum	protease	amino acids
fats	duodenum (from pancreas and intestinal juice)	lipase	fatty acids and glycerol

The need for chemical digestion

Most foods contain starch, protein and fat. These *large, insoluble molecules* cannot be absorbed into the blood stream so they need to be broken down into *small*, *soluble* and *absorbable* (diffusible) ones. *Glucose*, *amino acids*, *fatty acids* and *glycerol* all represent the smallest forms of their 'parent' molecules.

Teeth

There are *two sets* of teeth in a person's lifetime. The first set (or *milk* teeth) last for around 10–12 years before they are pushed out by the *permanent* teeth.

In the permanent set as shown in Figure 2.11, there are four types of tooth:

1. **Incisors:** There are *two* incisors in the front of each quarter-jaw.* They are sharp spade-like teeth for biting and cutting food. They are single-rooted.

NOTE

The molar teeth are part of the permanent set only — there are no 'milk molars'.

NOTE

*– A quarter-jaw is one half of the top jaw or bottom jaw.

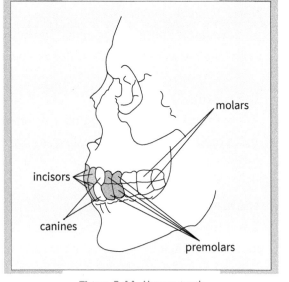

Figure 2.11 Human teeth

2. **Canines:** There is *one* canine per quarter-jaw. Although it is conical in shape, it is sharp and again used for biting and cutting food. They are single-rooted.

3. **Pre-molars:** There are *two* premolars per quarter-jaw. The surface of each tooth has two projections (cusps) which are used for crushing and grinding food. They are double-rooted teeth.

4. **Molars:** There are *three* molars per quarter-jaw (though the third molars – wisdom teeth – do not usually appear until the person is at least 17 years old). The tooth surface is square with four cusps again for crushing and grinding food. They are double-rooted teeth.

Mechanical digestion carried out by teeth is therefore ***biting, cutting, crushing*** and ***grinding*** (loosely called 'chewing').

The importance of proper tooth care

If teeth are not properly cared for, they may suffer from **dental caries** (or dental decay), the stages in which are as follows:

1. Food (particularly food containing sugar) becomes lodged between the teeth.

2. ***Bacteria*** settle in the sugary deposits, using them for their own metabolism.

3. The bacteria excrete ***acids*** which dissolve the outer non-living covering (enamel) of the tooth.

4. A cavity develops, in which more sugary deposits collect – attracting more bacteria. More excreted acids increase the size of the cavity.

5. Eventually, the decay reaches the living parts of the tooth – first the dentine where there are nerve endings and the tooth begins to ache. When decay reaches the pulp cavity it leads to an abscess.

Tooth structure and how it is affected by decay is shown in Figure 2.12.

Plaque

If the teeth remain uncleaned, a mixture of food, saliva, cheek cells and bacteria collect at the neck of the tooth (where it enters the gum). This deposit is called plaque. The acids released by the bacteria damage the enamel of the tooth in that region as well as cause gum disease.

NOTE

Although everyone has wisdom teeth, they sometimes remain below the gum and therefore not visible. They can also sometimes grow sideways into the neighbouring molar teeth, causing discomfort and pain. Such 'impacted wisdom teeth' may have to be surgically removed.

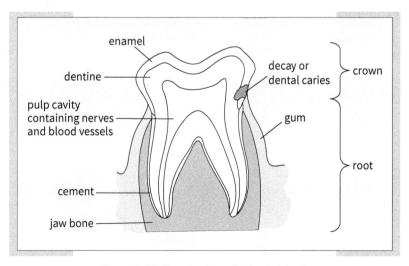

Figure 2.12 The structure of a (molar) tooth

Tartar

If not removed, plaque hardens to form tartar (or 'calculus'). This forms a solid protection for the bacteria trapped between it and the tooth allowing them to decay the tooth without interference.

How to care for teeth

1. Do not eat sweet (or starchy) foods before going to bed. (Saliva flow stops when we are asleep preventing the sugar from being washed away.) It is better to eat a raw crunchy food such as a carrot.
2. Brush the teeth last thing at night and first thing in the morning. Careful brushing removes plaque.
3. Use dental floss regularly to remove fragments of food from between the teeth.
4. Use a toothpaste which:
   a. contains fluoride to strengthen the tooth enamel
   b. contains a bactericide (to kill bacteria)
   c. is alkaline – to neutralise acids released by the bacteria.
5. Visit the dentist regularly for an examination (and have treatment if required).

The absorption and assimilation of food

The villi

The villi of the ileum are specially adapted for the process of food absorption. They are:

* extremely **numerous** – increasing the internal surface area of the ileum
* very **thin-walled** (one cell thick)
* contain **blood capillaries** just beneath their walls
* contain special structures (**lacteals**) for absorbing fatty acids and glycerol
* able to **move** to bring themselves into close contact with food.

The structure and function of a villus are shown in Figure 2.13.

Amino acids and glucose, after absorption by the blood capillaries, are carried **directly** to the **liver** for the first stage of their

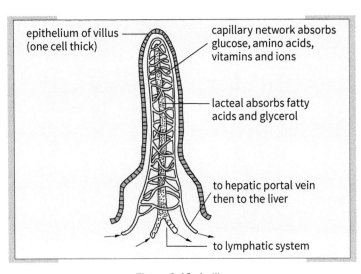

epithelium of villus (one cell thick)

capillary network absorbs glucose, amino acids, vitamins and ions

lacteal absorbs fatty acids and glycerol

to hepatic portal vein then to the liver

to lymphatic system

Figure 2.13 A villus

treatment in the body, by a blood vessel called the **hepatic portal vein**. Fats, after entering the lacteals, travel in the **lymphatic** system, by-passing the liver, and enter the circulatory system at a vein in the neck.

Assimilation

The main food substances, absorbed as small soluble molecules, must now be built up into the larger molecules needed by the body.

Glucose (and any other simple sugars which can be absorbed by the villi) may be used as it is as a substrate for **respiration** to release energy, but, after a meal, there will be more glucose available than is needed immediately for this purpose. It needs, therefore, to be **stored**. For this purpose, it is built up into a large insoluble molecule called **glycogen** (a polysaccharide, like starch). It is **stored** in the cells of the **liver** and **muscles** under the effect of the hormone **insulin** from the pancreas. Glucose still in excess is converted to starch and stored (in the skin and round the kidneys).

Amino acids are used in cells for building up **proteins** as the cells **grow**, and also for making special proteins such as **enzymes**. Amino acids (as well as proteins) are **never stored**. Any in excess to our needs at the time are broken down in the **liver** by a process called **deamination**.

Two separate molecules are produced as a result of deamination:
1. a **carbohydrate** which can be changed to glycogen and stored
2. **urea** (a **nitrogenous** waste product, i.e. one which contains nitrogen), which passes from the liver, in the blood, to the kidneys for excretion in **urine**.

The role of the liver in glucose and amino acid metabolism

The liver is involved in changing glucose to glycogen and storing it when blood glucose levels are high. It will also reconvert the glycogen to glucose and release the glucose into the blood when blood glucose levels are low. The liver is thus involved in the **regulation of blood glucose levels**. It also removes excess amino acids from the blood by deamination.

Note: Another major function of the liver is **detoxification** (the removal and breakdown of poisons – **toxins** – from the blood). One such toxin is alcohol. Although the liver is able to remove small quantities of alcohol, even on a regular basis, frequent high levels of alcohol in the blood can eventually lead to liver disease (**cirrhosis**).

Fat metabolism

The liver does not play a major part in fat metabolism. Once in the blood, fatty acids and glycerol recombine to form tiny fat droplets. (Fats at body temperature are in liquid form and thus the word lipid is better used to cover both fats and oils.)

The fat/lipid is stored in special storage cells:
1. in the skin ('adipose' tissue), and
2. around the kidneys.

It is a good insulator against **physical damage** and **low temperature**, and is a very efficient **energy store**, but it is heavy and leads to obesity.

Points to remember

* Know how plants obtain their water and their carbon dioxide for photosynthesis, and know the terms for all the **structural features of a leaf**.

* Be able to state the **equation** for **photosynthesis**, either in words on in symbols. If in symbols, then the equation **must balance**.

* Be able to describe the **experiments** that support this equation.

* Make sure you know the differences in chemical structure between **carbohydrates, fats** and **proteins** and that you know how to carry out **food tests** for each of these chemicals (and what results you would obtain).

* Learn the **constituents** of a healthy **diet**, be able to state a source for each one, and know their functions in the body.

* Know the **parts**, with their **functions**, of the alimentary canal.

* Know where **amylase, protease** and **lipase** are produced, where they are found and what their functions are in the alimentary canal.

* Know the structural features of a tooth, and how to care for your teeth.

Exam-style questions for you to try

1. Which of the following chemicals contains nitrogen?

   A. amino acid

   B. fat

   C. glucose

   D. starch

2. Which food test requires the use of heat?

   A. the test for fat

   B. the test for protein

   C. the test for reducing sugar

   D. the test for starch

3. Which condition is the result of a lack of vitamin C in the diet?

   A. anaemia

   B. bleeding gums

   C. constipation

   D. soft bones

4. Different tissues in a leaf contain different numbers of chloroplasts. Which gives these tissues in the correct sequence, starting with the tissue with the greatest number of chloroplasts?

   A. lower epidermis, palisade mesophyll, spongy mesophyll, upper epidermis

   B. upper epidermis, lower epidermis, spongy mesophyll, palisade mesophyll

   C. spongy mesophyll, palisade mesophyll, upper epidermis, lower epidermis

   D. palisade mesophyll, spongy mesophyll, lower epidermis, upper epidermis

5. The diagram shows a stage in the starch test on a leaf.

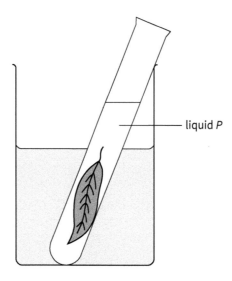

liquid *P*

What is liquid *P*?

A. boiling water

B. cold water

C. iodine solution

D. methylated spirits

6. Table 2.1 shows the masses of various substances in 100 g of banana fruit and in 100 g of avocado fruit.

substance	banana	avocado
fat	0.33 g	14.60 g
cholesterol	0.00 g	0.00 g
carbohydrate	22.80 g	8.53 g
fibre	2.60 g	6.70 g
protein	1.10 g	2.00 g
calcium	5.00 mg	12.00 mg
iron	0.26 mg	0.55 mg
vitamin C	8.70 mg	10.00 mg

Table 2.1

Table 2.2 shows a person's recommended daily intake for calcium, iron and vitamin C.

calcium	500 mg
iron	13 mg
vitamin C	62 mg

Table 2.2

Bananas form a significant part of the diet of some communities.

(a) Explain why bananas can be a valuable part of a person's diet.

....

....

....

....

.... [4]

(b) Explain why a diet of only bananas is not suitable for a growing child.

....

....

....

.... [3]

(c) Explain which of the two fruits, banana or avocado, it would be better to eat just before running a race.

....

....

....

.... [3]

Cambridge O Level Biology 5090 Paper 22 Q2 June 2011

7. Explain the importance to a plant of

   (a) the distribution of its chloroplasts

   ....

   ....

   ....

   ....

   ....

   .... [4]

   (b) the presence of stomata

   ....

   ....

   ....

   ....

   .... [3]

   (c) the position of its vascular bundles

   ....

   ....

   ....

   ....

   .... [3]

   Cambridge O Level Biology 5090 Paper 22 Q6 November 2011

NOTE

You may need to look at
Chapter 3 to help you a
little with Question 7 (c).

3 Transport

Chemicals are moved around living organisms. Here there is a description of the movement of water, ions, sugars and amino acids within a plant (involving transpiration and translocation). This is followed by a description of the human circulatory system and of the constituents of blood.

Transport in flowering plants

The transport system of a flowering plant has to provide a means of carrying **water** and **ions from the roots to the leaves**, and of carrying **sugars** and **amino acids from the leaves** to other parts of the plant while it is photosynthesising, and, if necessary, **from storage organs to the leaves** when it is not. Although glucose is the sugar made during photosynthesis, it is usually rapidly converted to starch and stored – first in the chloroplasts. If it is then moved around the plant, it is changed to **sucrose** in which form it is conducted through the **phloem** – usually to be converted back to starch when it reaches the storage organs.

Vascular bundles contain the tissues for transport – **xylem** for carrying **water and ions** and **phloem** for carrying **sugar (sucrose) and amino acids.**

The movement of sugar and amino acids around a plant is called **translocation.**

The positions occupied by xylem and phloem in the vascular bundles of roots, stems and leaves in a typical dicotyledonous plant are shown in Figure 3.1.

 NOTE

It will help you to remember what is carried in the xylem and phloem if you think of the three consecutive letters of the alphabet 'W, X and Y', standing for **W**ater in the **Xy**lem. Phloem carries the plant's food substances sugar and amino acids (**Ph**loem carries the plants **Ph**ood!).

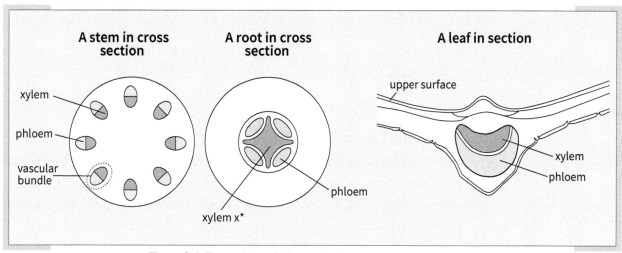

Figure 3.1 The position of xylem and phloem in a stem, root and leaf
*(A memory aid: 'x' for xylem marks the centre of a circle.)

Xylem is in the form of long tubes held open by having their walls **strengthened** with the chemical lignin. We are more familiar with lignin and its strength in the form of wood. Lignified xylem vessels therefore also:

1. help **support** the stem and photosynthesising tissues of the leaf
2. resist forces on the root which might cause the plant to be pulled out of the ground.

Aim: **To show that water travels up a stem in the xylem**

Apparatus:
- a beaker
- food colouring
- a soft-stemmed dicotyledonous plant (e.g., a broad bean)

Method: Cut the plant stem about 1 cm above the root and place it in water containing food colouring and leave, as shown in Figure 3.2, for about 1 day. Remove the stem from the beaker and carefully cut it through 2 to 3 cm from its base.

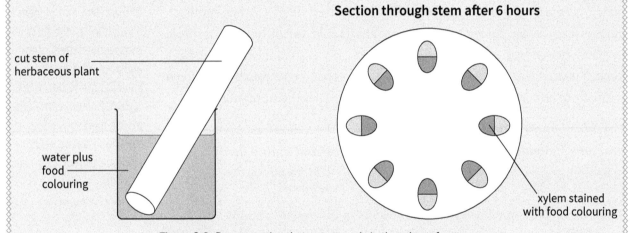

Figure 3.2 Demonstration that water travels in the xylem of a stem

Results: The vascular bundles will be seen to have been stained by the food colouring. If a very thin section is *carefully* cut from the stem, using a razor blade, and viewed under a microscope, it will be seen that the coloured region of the vascular bundle is in the position occupied by the *xylem*.

The path taken by water through a plant

In the section on osmosis the methods by which water enters **root hairs** were explained. Osmosis and diffusion also carry water across the root towards the xylem in the centre. This causes pressure (**root pressure**) forcing water into the xylem, and pushing it some way along the root towards the stem.

Once in the xylem of the stem, water is carried upwards by the second force at work – that of *capillarity*. This is the tendency for liquids to travel upwards through very narrow tubes (and can be demonstrated by dipping the end of very narrow capillary tubing in water). Xylem vessels have a microscopic bore which can be responsible for carrying water 20 or more centimetres up the plant.

The third force results from the evaporation of water from the mesophyll cells of the leaf and the removal of that water from the leaf through the stomata of the leaf. This process is *transpiration*, and it creates the force known as *transpiration pull* as it draws up more water to replace that which has been lost.

The three forces causing water to rise up a plant are therefore:
1. *root pressure*
2. *capillarity*
3. *transpiration pull*.

Transpiration pull, in particular, relies for its effectiveness on the fact that (water) molecules are attracted to one another and are thus not pulled apart as they move up the plant. These forces of 'molecular cohesion' ensure a continuous stream of water and ions travelling up the plant, known as the *transpiration stream*.

Transpiration

Transpiration is *the loss of water vapour from the leaves through the stomata.*

It occurs as follows:
1. Water leaves the xylem vessels in the leaf where if forms a water film on the walls of the mesophyll cells inside the leaf. This water film is for *dissolving carbon dioxide* for use during photosynthesis.

2. Water from the water film evaporates into the intercellular (leaf) spaces – greatly increasing the humidity of the air inside the leaf.

3. There is now a greater concentration of water vapour molecules inside the leaf than in the atmosphere outside, so they *diffuse* out *through the stomata* into the atmosphere.

So long as the stomata are open for the uptake of carbon dioxide, transpiration is bound to occur. If its rate *exceeds* that at which water can be absorbed from the soil, then water starts to be lost from the plant's cells. The cells *lose their turgidity* and the plant begins to *wilt*.

Conditions affecting the rate of transpiration

Those atmospheric conditions which affect the rate of evaporation of water also similarly affect the rate of transpiration. Thus,

transpiration speeded up by	transpiration slowed down by
dry air	humid air
high temperature	low temperature
air currents (wind)	still air
bright light*	dim light*

Although transpiration can lead to wilting, it also has the following **advantages**:
1. It maintains a constant supply of ions to the leaves.
2. It brings water to the mesophyll cells for photosynthesis.
3. It helps to supply water to all cells for metabolic processes and for turgidity.
4. It helps to cool leaves – important in very hot climates.

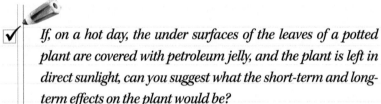

> ✔ *If, on a hot day, the under surfaces of the leaves of a potted plant are covered with petroleum jelly, and the plant is left in direct sunlight, can you suggest what the short-term and long-term effects on the plant would be?*

Transport in human beings

When applied to human beings, the term 'transport' system refers to the **circulatory system**. As in the flowering plant, it comprises a system of tubes. However, unlike the flowering plant, this time there is a **pump** (the heart) and a system of **valves** to ensure that the liquid within the tubes (**blood**) flows through them in **only one direction**.

Double (or dual) circulation

During one complete circulation of the human (mammalian) body, blood travels twice through the heart.
1. Blood arrives at the heart from the other organs of the body, and then travels to the lungs.
2. From the lungs, blood travels back to the heart, and then to the other organs of the body.

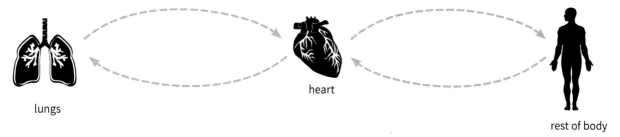

lungs   heart   rest of body

Figure 3.3 The double circulation of the blood

Figure 3.3 shows how blood arrives at the heart from the lungs, is pumped to the body, returns from the body, and is pumped back to the lungs.

The heart is completely divided into two halves in order to play its part in the dual circulation. One half deals with receiving deoxygenated blood from the body and pumping it to the lungs; the other half receives oxygenated blood from the lungs and sends it to the rest of the body.

Since the lungs lie either side of the heart, the distance the blood has to travel is short compared with how far it may travel into order to reach other parts of the body. Blood leaving the heart in the *lesser* circulation (to the lungs) is not under so much pressure as it is in the *greater* circulation. (Blood must always be able to reach the tissues of the finger tips, even when the arms are raised.)

The main blood vessels of the body

Blood always *leaves* the heart in *arteries*, which are vessels with thick muscular walls, able to withstand the high pressure of the blood. A large artery is called an *aorta*; a small one is called an *arteriole*.

Blood returning to the heart, under much lower pressure, does so in thinner-walled vessels called *veins*. A large vein is a *vena cava*: a small one is a *venule*.

Blood passes from arterioles to venules through microscopic blood vessels called *capillaries*.

Blood travels round the body as follows:

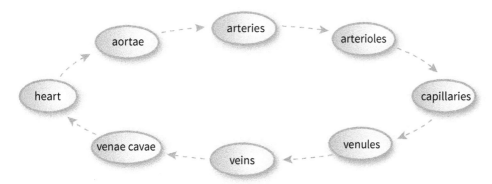

Figure 3.4 shows the names of the blood vessels associated with some of the main organs of the body.

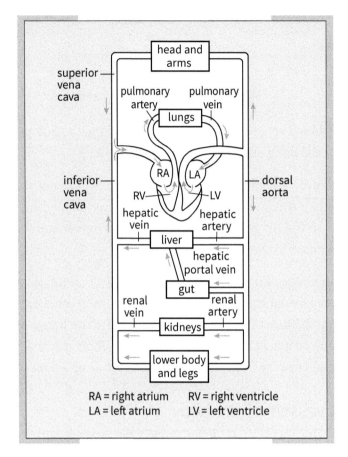

Figure 3.4 The mammalian circulatory system

The heart and how it functions

Important facts about the heart:

1. It is a ***muscular pump***.

2. It is made of special muscle ('cardiac' muscle) which has the ability to ***contract rhymically*** (even without stimulation).

3. It never tires or suffers from cramp.

4. It beats about 70 times per minute in the average adult at rest.

5. It has ***four*** chambers, all with similar volumes when full – ***two atria*** 'on top' (in mammals which walk upright) of ***two ventricles*** (see Figure 3.4).

6. Atria (singular atrium) have thin walls and receive the blood.

7. Ventricles have **thick** muscular walls to pump the blood out of the heart under pressure. The **left** ventricle having the thickest walls for sending blood round the body.

Structural features of the heart are shown in Figure 3.5.

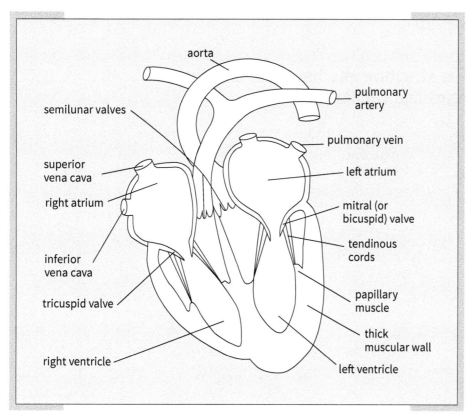

Figure 3.5 The mammalian heart

8. A system of **valves** ensures **one way flow** of blood through the heart.

9. A wave of contraction (called **systole**) passes over the heart from atria to ventricles, it forces blood from the atria into the ventricles, then forces blood out of the ventricles. As the ventricles contract, the mitral and tricuspid valves are slammed shut causing the 'lubb' sound of the heart beat.

10. The heart muscle then relaxes (**diastole**). As the ventricles do so, the semilunar valves close to stop blood being drawn back into the ventricles, causing the 'dupp' sound. There is then a pause before the next cycle of systole–diastole (and the next 'lubb-dupp' of the heart).

Each beat of the heart creates a surge of pressure in the arteries called the *pulse*. There is no such surge in the veins where blood flows smoothly under much lower pressure. Veins, however, have *semilunar valves* which prevent back-flow and ensure that blood continues to flow back towards the heart, but, otherwise, veins rely on the movement of nearby muscles (e.g., the calf muscles of the leg) to 'massage' the blood from one set of semilunar valves to the next.

The structure and functions of arteries, veins and capillaries

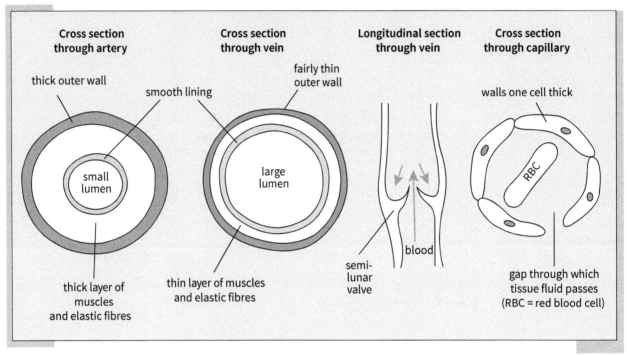

Figure 3.6 A comparison of blood vessels

Blood circulation is maintained by
* the force of contraction of the ventricles of the heart
* the muscles and elastic fibres in the arteries that prevent the arteries from ballooning as the pulse beat passes (a 'recoil' effect)
* valves in veins that prevent backflow
* the contraction of skeletal muscles near veins which help to push the blood from one set of valves to the next
* the 'suction' (reduced pressure) caused each time the heart relaxes.

A comparison of the three types of blood vessel

The differences in structure and function between arteries, veins and capillaries are shown in Figure 3.6, and the differences in their functions are given below.

arteries	veins	capillaries
take blood *from* the heart	take blood *to* the heart	take blood from arteries to veins
blood under **high** pressure	blood under **low** pressure	blood pressure rises then gradually falls as blood flows from arteries to veins
blood flows in pulses	blood flows smoothly – **no** pulse	pulse gradually disappears
thick muscular walls with narrow lumen*	thinner walls with wide lumen	wall one cell thick, leaky and red blood cells travel in single file
no semilunar valves (except the pulmonary artery and the aorta)	semilunar vales present	no semilunar valves
carry oxygenated blood (except the pulmonary artery)	carry de-oxygenated blood (except the pulmonary vein)	blood slowly loses its oxygen

NOTE

*The lumen is the hole through which the blood passes along the blood vessel.

The pulse beat in an artery can be located by gently pressing on the wrist at the base of the thumb using your middle and index fingers as shown in Figure 3.7.

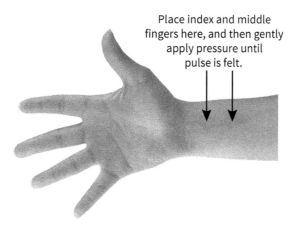

Place index and middle fingers here, and then gently apply pressure until pulse is felt.

Figure 3.7 Counting the pulse

The number of pulse beats in one minute can be counted, but it is more usual to count the number of beats in a shorter period of time – say 15 seconds – and then calculate the rate per minute.

✓ *Can you suggest why blood samples for medical purposes are usually taken from veins rather than arteries?*

Aim:	**To investigate the effect of physical activity on pulse rate**
Apparatus:	A stop watch/clock or a clock with a sweep seconds hand.
Method:	The number of pulse beats is counted over three separate minutes. Each result is recorded and an ***average*** taken. The pulse rate of a person is taken by counting the number of beats in one minute, and recorded. About 5 minutes exercise is performed (e.g., running, or stepping on and off a stair step).
	The number of pulse beats in 10 seconds is counted and recorded, then, after 20 seconds, the number of beats is again counted over a 10-second period. The process is continued for 10 minutes. Each recorded number is multiplied by 6 to obtain the rate per minute. These figures can then be used to draw a graph of the rate against time to show how the rate of heartbeat gradually returns to normal after exercise. The fitter the subject, the quicker the pulse rate returns to normal.
Results:	As shown in Figure 3.8, the pulse rate rises considerably and then takes several minutes to return to its original level.

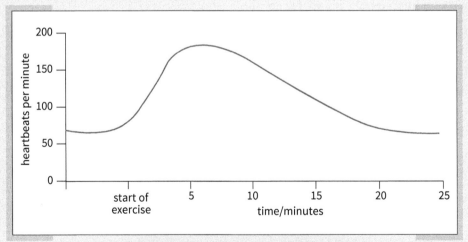

Figure 3.8 The effect of exercise on pulse rate

Conclusion:	Exercise requires more oxygen to be sent to the muscles and more carbon dioxide to be removed from them. The heart beats faster, increasing the rate of circulation allowing oxygen and carbon dioxide to be supplied and removed at a faster rate. The pulse rate takes some time to return to its original level as the waste products of muscle action take some time to be broken down (oxidised).

Try sitting quietly with one leg crossed over the other. You should be able to see the foot of the leg that is now on top making a slight 'kicking' movement each time blood is forced along the main artery of that leg.

Heart disease

To keep the heart healthy, diet is important. Like all muscles, the heart benefits from exercise if it is to continue to work efficiently. Apart from the effects of atheroma, the **coronary artery** may carry insufficient blood to the heart muscle if a person smokes (since **carbon monoxide** in cigarette smoke reduces the amount of oxygen carried by haemoglobin, and nicotine in cigarette smoke increases the tendency for **blood to clot**). Blockage of a blood vessel is called **occlusion**.

People who lead **stressful** lives are also at risk of heart disease, since stress causes the release of raised levels of the hormone **adrenaline** which has the effect of constricting the arteries by contacting muscles in the artery walls which may already be partially blocked.

To **decrease** the risk of heart disease, therefore:
* restrict the intake of animal fats and cholesterol
* avoid obesity
* do not smoke
* settle for a less stressful lifestyle
* take regular exercise.

See reference to diet and heart disease.

Blood

Structural features and functions of the individual components of blood (as shown in Figure 3.9)

Red blood cells

Structure
* They are **biconcave discs**.
* They are extremely small (2 μm × 7 μm).
* They have **no nucleus**.
* They live for **only 120 days**.
* They are made in the bone marrow.
* They are destroyed in the liver.
* Their cytoplasm contains the red **iron**-containing protein called **haemoglobin**.

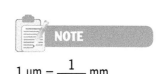

$1 \ \mu m = \dfrac{1}{1000} \ mm$

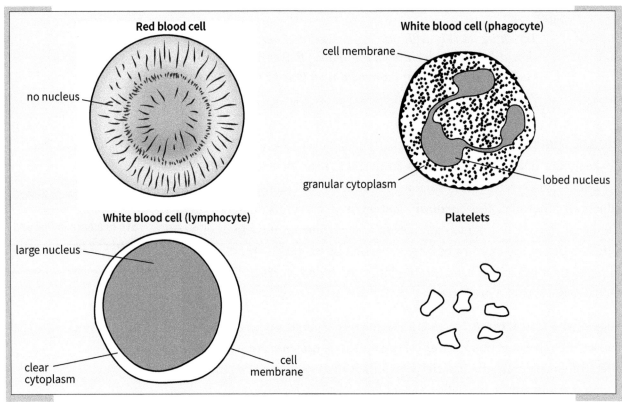

Figure 3.9 Blood

* They are flexible allowing them to pass through the very narrow capillaries.
* There are 4–5 000 000 RBCs per mm³ of blood.

Function

They carry out the **uptake** and **carriage of oxygen**, by the **haemoglobin** in the form of **oxyhaemoglobin**.

White blood cells

There are two types of white blood cells:

1. **phagocytes**   2. **lymphocytes**

Structure of phagocytes

* They are about 10 µm in diameter.
* They have a **lobed nucleus**.
* They are made in the bone marrow.
* They are capable of movement ('amoeboid' movement), and can squeeze out of capillaries.
* There are about 5000 per mm³ of blood.

Function of phagocytes

They carry out **phagocytosis**, i.e. they **ingest** potentially harmful **bacteria**, thus preventing or overcoming infection.

Structure of lymphocytes

* They, too, are about 10 μm in diameter.
* They have a **large round nucleus** occupying almost the entire cell.
* They are made in **lymph nodes** (see later in the chapter).
* There are about 2000 per mm³ of blood.

Function of lymphocytes

They produce **antibodies**, which are proteins that 'stick' to bacteria and clump them together ready for being ingested by phagocytes. Some antibodies are in the form of **antitoxins**, which neutralise poisons (toxins) in the blood which have been released by invading bacteria.

Antibodies are specific to the organism against which they are produced. They may stay in the blood only for a few weeks, or for a lifetime – giving life-long immunity against the effects of that particular disease-causing agent (or **pathogen**).

Tissue rejection

Since our immune system is unable to distinguish between possibly harmful protein, as in pathogenic bacteria, and potentially useful 'foreign' protein, as in a transplanted heart or kidney, there is always a danger of **tissue rejection** when a transplant operation is carried out. The more similar the protein structure in the transplanted organ is to the proteins of the recipient, the less likely are the chances of rejection. Organs, therefore, from a (close) relative are far less likely to be rejected, because the protein types will have a greater similarity.

Platelets

Structure

1. They are fragments of cells.
2. They are made in bone marrow.
3. There are 250 000 per mm³ of blood.

Function

They play a part in **blood clotting** and help to block holes in damaged capillary walls.

NOTE

'Ingest' is the correct term. You can also use the term 'engulf' but never 'eat' or 'fight'.

NOTE

If a minor injury to your skin is not carefully cleaned, it may become infected with bacteria. White blood cells arriving at the injury may be killed by the toxins released by the bacteria. They then form a part of the pus (dead cells) that collects around the wound.

Plasma

Structure

1. It is a pale yellow watery fluid.
2. It contains the following *in solution*:

    * digested foods (*amino acids, glucose*)
    * vitamins
    * ions (salts)
    * excretory materials (*urea, carbon dioxide*)
    * hormones
    * plasma (or 'blood') proteins (e.g., antibodies and *fibrinogen*)

    and also:

    * fat droplets (in suspension)
    * heat
    * red and white blood cells and platelets.

Function

The plasma carries all the materials from where they are absorbed or produced, to the parts of the body where they are needed or excreted (e.g., carbon dioxide from the cells of the body to the lungs).

How substances in the capillaries reach the cells of the body

Since the walls of capillaries leak, some, but not all, of the materials in the plasma can escape. The blood cells are too large to leave the capillaries (though the phagocytes are able, by their own efforts, to squeeze out between the cells in the capillary walls). Most plasma protein molecules are too large to pass out of the capillaries. All the smaller molecules in solution pass out as shown in Figure 3.10, to bathe the cells in what is known as *tissue fluid*.

Tissue fluid is, therefore, blood *minus* red blood cells, plasma proteins and some white blood cells.

NOTE

Fibrinogen is a soluble protein, which, when in contact with enzymes released by damaged cells, is converted into an insoluble, stringy protein called fibrin. This forms a mesh which traps blood cells and becomes a clot – preventing the entry of bacteria. The clot dries and hardens to form a scab which covers the wound until the skin beneath has repaired.

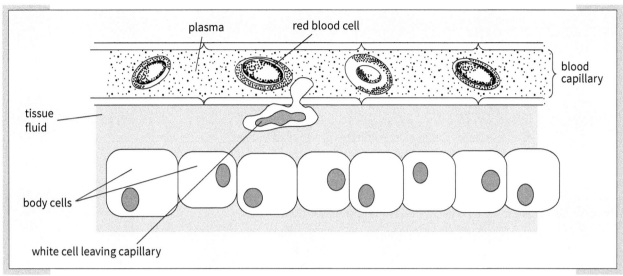

Figure 3.10 The relationship between blood, tissue fluid and body cells

Tissue fluid is then collected into a system of vein-like vessels called **lymphatic vessels** which take the tissue fluid and return it to the circulatory system via a vein in the neck. In certain places in the lymphatic system, e.g., the neck and armpit, there are structures called lymph nodes that manufacture lymphocytes.

If you suffer a graze to your arm in which only the very top layers of skin are removed, the wound 'weeps' a clear yellowish fluid rather than red blood. Can you explain this?

Points to remember

* Make sure you know that evaporation occurs **inside** the leaf, and then water vapour diffuses out through the stomata during transpiration.

* Know the difference between **xylem** and **phloem**, what each of them carries and where they are found in the different plant organs.

* Be clear on the differences between **transpiration** and **translocation.**

* Learn the difference between the pulmonary artery and the pulmonary vein.

* Know which valves open and which close at the different stages of a heart cycle.

* Know the differences in structure and function of blood cells.

* Know the difference between **blood plasma** and **tissue fluid**.

Exam-style questions for you to try

1. What is meant by the term 'dual circulation'?

    A. A blood cell passes through the heart twice in one complete circulation.

    B. Blood travels twice round the body before being pumped to the lungs.

    C. The heart contains two different types of valve.

    D. There are two types of chambers in the heart, atria and ventricles.

2. Figure 3.11 shows a section through the heart (viewed from the front). Which valve closes in order to ensure that blood flows to the lungs?

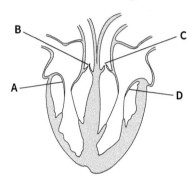

Figure 3.11

3. Which chemical is carried in the phloem?

    A. glucose

    B. nitrate

    C. starch

    D. sucrose

4. How are stomata related to the movement of water?

    A. Water enters through them as water vapour.

    B. Water enters through them in liquid form.

    C. Water leaves through them as water vapour.

    D. Water leaves through them in liquid form.

5. Which shows substances that pass from a capillary to a nearby body cell?

	amino acids	blood proteins	glucose	urea
A	✓	✓	✗	✗
B	✓	✗	✓	✗
C	✗	✓	✗	✓
D	✗	✗	✓	✓

6. Figure 3.12 shows an experiment on the uptake of water by a leafy shoot. The black cover is placed over the leafy shoot for 30 minutes.

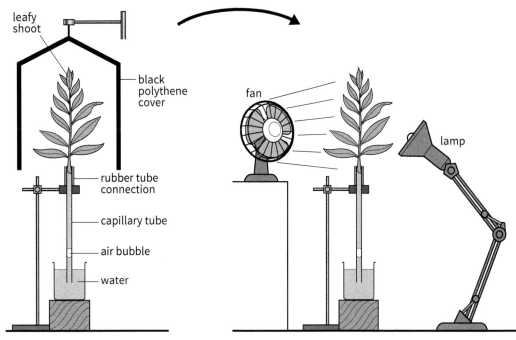

Figure 3.12

(a) State what is likely to happen to the air bubble in the capillary tube after 30 minutes.

.... [1]

(b) The black polythene cover is then removed from the plant. A fan and a lamp are placed either side of the plant and both are switched on.

State what effect this will have on the bubble in the capillary tube

.... [2]

(c) Explain how each of the following effect the movement of the bubble:

(i) the fan

....

....

....

(ii) the removal of the polythene cover

....

....

....

(iii) the lamp

....

....

....[8]

7. Describe how blood is made to flow in a continuous circulation around the body with reference to

(a) the heart

....

....

....

....

....

....[4]

(b) the arteries

....

....

....

....

....[3]

(c) the veins

....

....

....

....

.... [3]

Cambridge O Level Biology 5090 paper 22 Q7 November 2011

8. Figure 3.13 shows the loss in dry mass of leaves, as a result of translocation and respiration, with increasing temperature. The light intensity is kept constant.

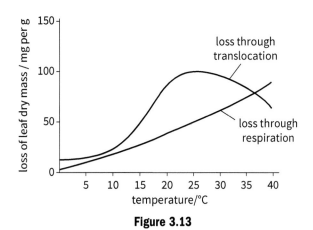

Figure 3.13

(a) State the chemical compound that is responsible for the loss in dry mass through translocation, and name the tissue in which it is carried.

compound

....

tissue

.... [2]

(b) Using Figure 3.13, state the temperature at which there is the greatest total loss of dry mass, and calculate the loss of dry mass at that temperature.

temperature

....

total loss of dry mass

.... [3]

(c) Explain the cause of the loss of dry mass as a result of respiration.

....

....

....

....

....

.... [4]

(d) Suggest and explain the effect of increasing the light intensity on the results shown in Figure 3.13.

....

....

....

....

....

.... [4]

9. Figure 3.14 shows part of the circulatory system, and the positions in which blood samples were taken in order to assess the content of blood gases in different parts of a patient's body.

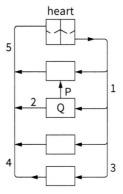

Figure 3.14

Table 3.1 shows the results that were obtained.

sample point	cm³ gas per 100 cm³ of blood		
	carbon dioxide	oxygen	nitrogen
1	49	19	1
2	52	16	1
3	49	19	1
4	54	16	1
5	56	12	1

(a) Name blood vessel P and organ Q

P .... Q .... [2]

(b) Explain why the content of nitrogen in the blood remains constant.

.... [2]

(c) Explain why sample 5 still contains oxygen.

....

....

....

.... [3]

(d) Describe how blood travels from point 5 to point 1 and how the structures it passes through account for the changes in its gas content.

....

....

....

....

....

....

.... [5]

4 Life Processes

This chapter deals with respiration, excretion and homeostasis. There is an account of how oxygen gets into the blood and how carbon dioxide is removed from it. There is also an account of kidney dialysis. The concept of a negative feedback system is described. An account of coordination is given, first involving the nervous system, reflex actions and the structure of the eye, then involving hormonal control. The chapter ends with a consideration of support and locomotion.

 ## Respiration

Respiration is a characteristic of **all** living organisms. **It is the release of energy from food substances in all living cells.** The food substance is usually glucose.

There are two forms of respiration.

Aerobic respiration

Aerobic respiration may be defined *as the release of relatively large amounts of energy by the breakdown of food substances in the presence of oxygen.*

Aerobic respiration usually takes the form of the **oxidation of glucose** in the cytoplasm of living cells, controlled by **enzymes**. It unlocks the chemical energy in the glucose molecule, releasing it for metabolic activities, and releasing also the waste products **carbon dioxide** and **water**.

$$C_6H_{12}O_6 + 6O_2 \longrightarrow 6CO_2 + 6H_2O + \text{energy released}$$

(glucose)　(oxygen)　　　　　(carbon　　(water)　　　　(16.1 kJ/g
　　　　　　　　　　　　　dioxide)　　　　　　　　　glucose)

The energy that is released may be used in the following ways:

1. for **muscle contraction** (bringing about movement and locomotion)
2. to help link together amino acids in order to **manufacture proteins** (such as enzymes and those used for growth and repair)
3. for **cell division**
4. for **active transport** of chemicals through cell membranes (e.g., the uptake of glucose through the villus walls)
5. conversion into **electrical** energy in the form of **impulses** along nerve cells
6. conversion into **heat** energy to **maintain a constant body temperature**.

 NOTE

Never say that respiration 'produces' or 'makes' energy. **Only** the Sun does that.

Anaerobic respiration

Anaerobic respiration is a form of respiration in which relatively small amounts of energy are released by the breakdown of food substances in the absence of oxygen.

It is the process by which **yeast** cells break down **glucose** during **fermentation** to produce **ethanol** (alcohol).

$$C_6H_{12}O_6 \longrightarrow 2C_2H_5OH + 2CO_2 + \text{some energy released}$$

(glucose)   (ethanol)   (carbon   (1.17 kJ/g glucose)
dioxide)

Less energy is released than in aerobic respiration since the alcohol molecule is relatively large and still contains a considerable amount of chemical energy.

Anaerobic respiration also occurs in the **human body** especially in **muscles**. It happens when there is not enough oxygen reaching the cells for aerobic respiration to meet the energy demands of the body and it occurs especially during exercise when energy demands are high. Instead, the glucose is partially broken down, without oxygen, to **lactic acid**, with only a limited amount of energy being released.

$$C_6H_{12}O_6 \longrightarrow 2C_3H_6O_3 + \text{some energy released}$$

(glucose)   (lactic acid)   (0.83 kJ/g glucose)

NOTE

If the circulation is inefficient, high levels of lactic acid in the muscles may lead to **cramp**.

The circulatory system carries the lactic acid away from the muscle to the liver where it is oxidised to carbon dioxide and water, but this happens **after the period of exercise has finished**. The oxygen used for this process is said to be used to pay off the **oxygen debt**.

Gaseous exchange in the human

Oxygen enters the blood from the lungs. In order to move air containing oxygen from the atmosphere to the exchange surfaces of the lungs, a muscular, pumping action called **breathing** must occur. Breathing in (**inspiration**) is responsible for presenting air with its oxygen to the surfaces where gaseous exchange will take place. **Expiration** pushes the air, now containing waste carbon dioxide, back into the atmosphere (breathing out).

The differences between inspired and expired air

inspired air	expired air
21% oxygen	16% oxygen
0.04% carbon dioxide	4% carbon dioxide
relatively dry	saturated
at air temperature	at body temperature
relatively dirty	relatively clean
78% nitrogen	though the same *amount* of nitrogen is breathed out as is breathed in, its percentage of the air breathed out actually falls since there is a greater concentration of water vapour in expired air and water vapour is a gas

The following are practical demonstrations to show some of these differences.

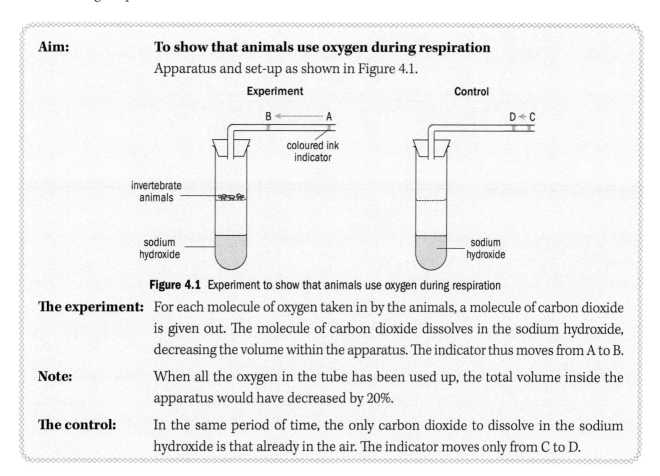

Aim: **To show that animals use oxygen during respiration**

Apparatus and set-up as shown in Figure 4.1.

Figure 4.1 Experiment to show that animals use oxygen during respiration

The experiment: For each molecule of oxygen taken in by the animals, a molecule of carbon dioxide is given out. The molecule of carbon dioxide dissolves in the sodium hydroxide, decreasing the volume within the apparatus. The indicator thus moves from A to B.

Note: When all the oxygen in the tube has been used up, the total volume inside the apparatus would have decreased by 20%.

The control: In the same period of time, the only carbon dioxide to dissolve in the sodium hydroxide is that already in the air. The indicator moves only from C to D.

Experiment to show that air breathed out contains more carbon dioxide than air breathed in.

Apparatus and set-up as shown in Figure 4.2

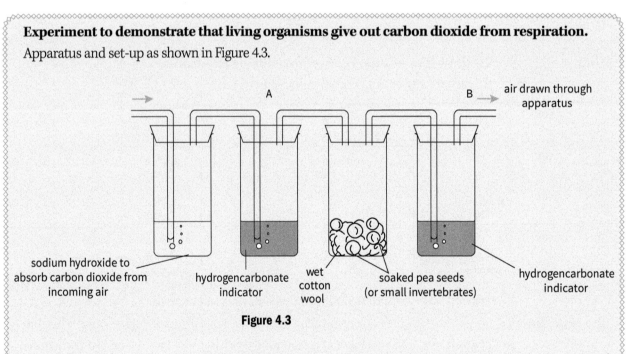

Person breathing gently

to mouth   from mouth

air in   air out

hydrogencarbonate indicator turns from red to orange to yellow in the presence of carbon dioxide

hydrogencarbonate indicator turns from red to orange

hydrogencarbonate indicator turns from red to yellow

Figure 4.2

Experiment to demonstrate that living organisms give out carbon dioxide from respiration.

Apparatus and set-up as shown in Figure 4.3.

A   B   air drawn through apparatus

sodium hydroxide to absorb carbon dioxide from incoming air

hydrogencarbonate indicator

wet cotton wool

soaked pea seeds (or small invertebrates)

hydrogencarbonate indicator

Figure 4.3

A   The hydrogencarbonate indicator remains red, showing that no carbon dioxide is passing on to the next tube.

B   The hydrogencarbonate indicator changes from red to yellow, showing that carbon dioxide is present. The carbon dioxide is evolved by the respiring peas.

Depending on the need for oxygen in the body (and the need to remove waste carbon dioxide), the **rate** and **depth** of breathing may vary.

More oxygen is used, and more carbon dioxide is released when we are active. This can be demonstrated as follows:

NOTE

Why measure the rate three times? Would once be acceptable? Is three times enough?

Aim: **To show the effect of exercise on the rate of breathing**

Count the number of breaths taken in one minute by a person at rest. (It is easier to count someone else's breathing rate than it is to count one's own.) Do this **three** times and take an average (around 15 breaths per minute).

Perform 5 minutes of exercise as when investigating pulse rate. Using the same procedure as then, count the number of breaths in a 10-second period every 30 seconds for 10 minutes.

Calculate the rate per minute, and plot a graph of breathing rate against time.

Aim: **To show the long-term effect of exercise on the depth of breathing**
Apparatus and set-up as shown in Figure 4.4

The taking of regular exercise can affect the volume of air a person is able to inspire and then expire in one deep breath. This can be demonstrated by using the simple respirometer shown below.

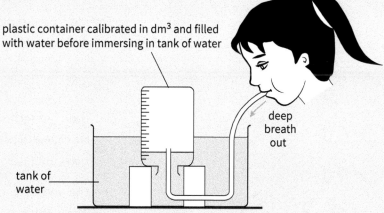

plastic container calibrated in dm³ and filled with water before immersing in tank of water

deep breath out

tank of water

Figure 4.4 Measurement of the effective lung volume

A group of athletes and a group of non-athletes can, in turn, breathe in as far as they can, and then breathe out through the rubber tube as far as they can. Measure, in each case, the volume of water expelled from the container. The container will need to be refilled with water after each deep breath out. An average per person for the athletes and for the non-athletes can be calculated, and the results compared. Athletes will be likely to be able to exhale a greater volume of air (and thus, be able to breathe more deeply).

The effect of exercise on breathing rate and depth

The *immediate* effect of exercise on the depth of breathing may be successfully demonstrated only with a commercial respirometer, where the person breathes in and out through a tube connected to a piece of electronic equipment which provides a graph of the depth (as well as the frequency) of breathing. A graph similar to the one shown below (Figure 4.5) would be expected if a person measured the depth and rate of breathing before and every 30 seconds after a period of exercise.

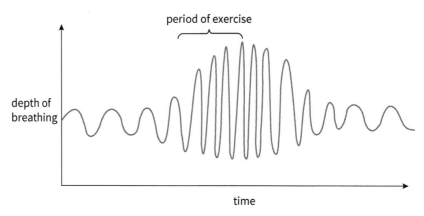

Figure 4.5 Graph showing the effect of exercise on the rate and depth of breathing.

The structure of the respiratory organs

A pair of *lungs* lies in the (airtight) *thoracic* (chest) *cavity*, as shown in Figure 4.6.

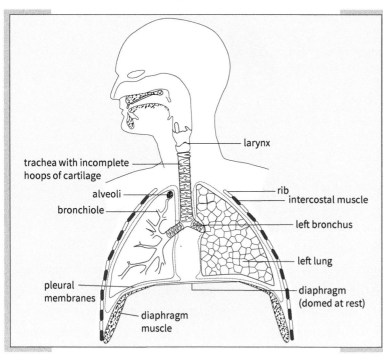

Figure 4.6 The respiratory organs

During breathing, the lungs are inflated and deflated by the action of muscles which help to form the thorax. They are:

1. the *external* and *internal intercostal muscles* (between the ribs), and

2. the muscles of the *diaphragm.* The diaphragm is a sheet of muscle lying below the lungs, separating them from the abdomen. When relaxed, it is curved upwards (towards the lungs) like a dome.

These muscles work to alter the **volume** of the thoracic cavity, which, in turn, alters the **pressure** within the thoracic cavity.

During inspiration:
1. The (external) ***intercostal muscles contract***. This causes the ribs to swing **up** and **out** – increasing the volume of the thorax ('front' to 'back').
2. The muscles of the ***diaphragm contract***, pulling it ***flat*** – increasing further the volume of the thorax (this time 'top' to 'bottom').

The resultant increase in volume of the thorax ***decreases its pressure***.

The only connection between the thorax and the higher pressure of the outside atmosphere is via the mouth and nose, so air from the atmosphere is ***forced*** towards the region of lower pressure. It passes through the nose and/or mouth, down the ***trachea***, through the ***bronchi*** and ***bronchioles*** and into the ***alveoli***. Gaseous exchange then occurs.

How air is cleaned before entering the lungs

The trachea ***is lined with ciliated cells*** and goblet cells. Goblet cells secrete mucus, a sticky fluid containing protein that traps bacteria and dust particles as they pass in inhaled (breathed in) air. The mucus is then carried towards the throat by the ***upward-beating*** microscopic projections (***cilia***) of the ciliated cells (See Figure 4.7.).

The mucus, plus dust particles and bacteria are then swallowed. Many of the bacteria will perish when they meet the stomach acid. In this way, the lungs are protected against many harmful (pathogenic) bacteria.

During expiration:
1. The (external) intercostal muscles **relax** – the ribs **swing down** and **in** (largely under gravitational force).
2. The diaphragm muscles **relax** and the diaphragm **domes upwards** again.

NOTE

Avoid saying that air is 'sucked'. It is the higher pressure that 'pushes' the air.

NOTE

Remember that the cilia do not act as filters for dust and bacteria.

NOTE

This is sometimes described as a 'moving carpet' of mucus.

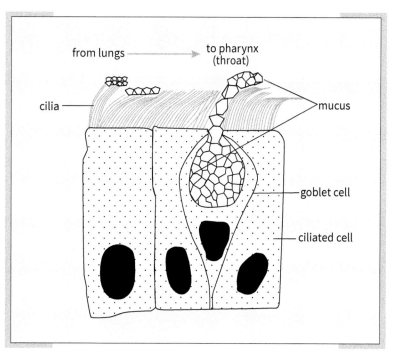

Figure 4.7 Cilia lining the trachea

Intercostal means 'between' (inter) 'the ribs' (costal).

These actions **decrease** the volume of the thoracic cavity, **increasing** its pressure. Air is **forced** back out into the atmosphere.

Although gravity helps the ribs to swing down and in during expiration, there are also **internal** intercostal muscles, which **relax** during inspiration and **contract** during **expiration** to help provide some additional force to the action of expiration.

It is estimated that the alveoli provide the lungs with a surface area roughly the same as a doubles tennis court.

How alveoli are adapted for the process of gaseous exchange

* The millions of alveoli provide a **large surface area** for gaseous exchange.
* The walls of the alveoli are covered with a layer of **water** to dissolve the gases.
* The walls are only **one cell thick** for quick and easy **diffusion** of gases in solution.
* They are richly supplied with **capillaries** for rapid transport of the gases.

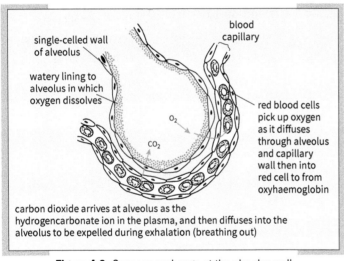

single-celled wall of alveolus

watery lining to alveolus in which oxygen dissolves

blood capillary

O_2

CO_2

red blood cells pick up oxygen as it diffuses through alveolus and capillary wall then into red cell to from oxyhaemoglobin

carbon dioxide arrives at alveolus as the hydrogencarbonate ion in the plasma, and then diffuses into the alveolus to be expelled during exhalation (breathing out)

Figure 4.8 Gaseous exchange at the alveolus wall

 **Excretion**

The metabolic reactions within the body are always creating waste products.

Excretion is defined as **the removal of toxic material from organisms, and the waste products of metabolism (chemical reactions in the cells including respiration)**.

There are two main sets of excretory organs for removing metabolic waste products, the **lungs** and the **kidneys**.

The sweat glands in the skin also remove a little urea since it is one of the constituents of sweat.

excretory organ	material removed	method of removal
the kidneys	urea	in urine
	salts and toxins	in urine
the lungs	carbon dioxide	breathing out (exhalation)

The removal of faeces from the alimentary canal is **not** regarded as excretion, since the fibre which makes up the faeces is not the product of a chemical reaction in the body. Instead, it passed all the way through the intestines unaffected by any enzymes released. (However, the pigment which colours the faeces, which comes from the chemical breakdown of red blood cells, could be regarded as excretory.)

The lungs

The passage of carbon dioxide from the blood capillaries, its diffusion through the alveolus walls and then its removal from the body in expired air is described in Figure 4.8. Carbon dioxide is an **excretory** product since it is a waste product of respiration in the cells of the body.

The kidneys

The kidneys are two brown bean-shaped organs lying dorsally (i.e. towards the back) in the abdominal cavity. They are supplied with blood along the **renal artery** and return it to the rest of the circulation via the **renal vein**. Their job is to carry out **high pressure filtration** of the blood, during which **two** functions have to be achieved:

1. the removal of **urea** and **salts** and **toxins** from the blood (i.e. part of **excretion**)
2. the maintenance of a constant concentration of blood plasma (**osmoregulation**).

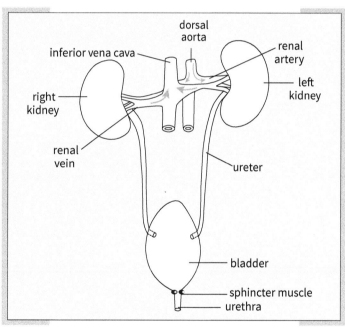

Figure 4.9 The excretory organs

Osmoregulation may be achieved either by the removal (if it is in excess) or the retention of **water**, or by the removal (if they are in excess) or the retention of **ions** (salts).

The materials removed from the blood by each kidney are then sent down the **ureter** to the (urinary) **bladder** where they are **stored**. Relaxation of the **bladder sphincter** muscle allows them to leave the body as a **solution** called **urine** via the **urethra**. Important structural features relating to the kidneys are shown in Figure 4.9.

urine ⟶ urea + ions + toxins + water

NOTE

Learn to spell 'ureter' and 'urethra' correctly – and know which is which.

NOTE

In the case of a diabetic person who has an excess of glucose in their blood, the kidneys will remove some of the excess glucose as well. In a healthy person, any glucose filtered from the blood is reabsorbed, along with some of the salts, from the kidney tissues back into the blood before the urine leaves the kidneys.

Kidney dialysis

If the kidneys fail, then there will be a build-up of urea and toxins in the blood which would eventually prove fatal. Subject to availability and suitability of tissue type, a **kidney transplant** may be possible. Otherwise, kidney dialysis (Figure 4.10) may be used. A **kidney dialysis machine** removes, from a patient's blood, chemicals with **small** molecules (urea, toxins and ions) but does not allow larger molecules (such as plasma proteins) to leave the blood.

This is achieved by passing the patient's blood through **dialysis tubing** which is **partially permeable**, i.e. permeable only to small molecules. This tubing is placed in a **washing fluid** which is continuously renewed, and which washes away the substances removed from the blood. These substances include **urea, excess salts** and **toxins**. By varying the concentration of substances in the washing fluid, the amounts of those substances which leave the blood (by **diffusion** down their **concentration gradient**) can be controlled. In this way, the concentration of the plasma in the blood is regulated before it is then returned to the patient.

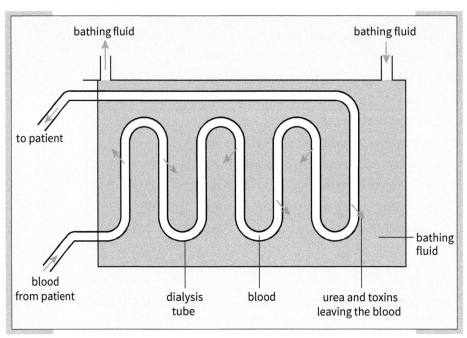

Figure 4.10 How an 'artificial kidney' works

 **Homeostasis**

The body will operate most efficiently only if conditions within it remain reasonably stable. As has been shown, the kidneys have the important function of keeping the blood plasma at a constant concentration. The tissue fluid bathing the body's cells is therefore always at a constant concentration. Because all cell membranes are partially permeable, and then osmosis will ensure that the concentration within all cells is also always constant and equal to that of the tissue fluid. Many organs within the body play a part in maintaining constant conditions, and are described as **organs of homeostasis**.

Homeostasis is defined as *the maintenance of a constant internal environment*.

The skin

The skin is the largest organ of the human body. Its structure is shown in Figure 4.11. It is an important **sense organ**, but also forms the barrier between the body and the external environment. It is the organ through which we may both gain and lose heat. This is particularly important in the **homeostatic** process of **temperature regulation**.

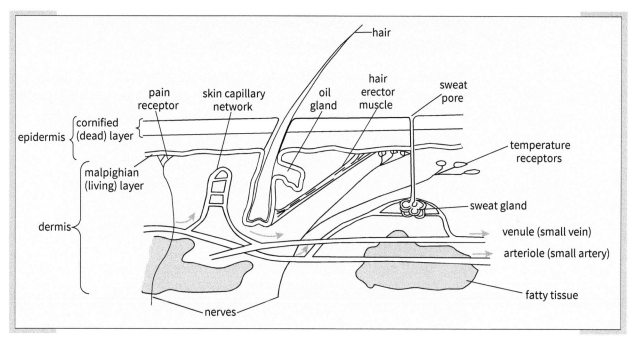

Figure 4.11 Mammalian skin

The part played by the skin in temperature regulation

The temperature of the skin surface, which depends on the environmental temperature as well as the blood temperature, is detected by the **temperature receptors** in the skin.

When the temperature of the blood **rises** above 37°C:

1. The **sweat glands** release more **sweat**.
2. The sweat **evaporates**.*
3. **Arterioles** in the skin **dilate** (become wider as their muscular walls relax, called vasodilation).
4. More blood is brought to the skin – blood carries heat.*

*Thus more heat is lost to the environment, cooling the blood and allowing the body temperature to return to normal.
The person may also take cold drinks, and seek shade.

When the temperature of the blood *falls* below 37°C:

1. Sweating is greatly reduced.*
2. Arterioles in the skin *constrict* (become narrower as their muscular walls contract and called vasoconstriction).
3. Less blood flows beneath the skin surface.*
4. *Fat* in the *dermis* of the skin acts as an *insulator.*

If the above measures prove inadequate, muscles in the body will start to contract and relax rhythmically. This is called *shivering*. It releases heat energy.

A person may take warm drinks, increase the insulating layer of air around the body by wearing more clothes, and do some exercise, all of which will help to raise body temperature.

Sweating is a process that does not 'start' when your body temperature rises above normal or 'stop' when the temperature falls below normal. Sweating is a continuous process that increases or decreases.

Capillaries in the skin do *not* move nearer to or further away from the skin as the temperature of the body changes. The muscles in the walls of the arterioles that supply the capillaries contract or relax. When they relax, more blood flows into the capillaries which therefore get wider (dilate). When the muscles in the arteriole walls contract, less blood flows into the capillaries, but it is the arterioles that constrict *not* the capillaries, as capillaries have no muscles in their walls.

Temperature receptors in the skin

As a sense organ, one of the properties of the skin is to be able to *detect temperature change in the external environment*. A change in atmospheric temperature will thus start some of the temperature control mechanisms, even before there is any significant change in the temperature of the blood.

Changes in the blood temperature are detected by the *hypothalamus* situated on the under-side of the *brain*. This is the structure responsible for the *coordination* of all the temperature control mechanisms.

The concept of control by negative feedback

In order to maintain a constant internal environment, it is necessary to have *receptors* ('sensors') in the body capable of detecting when the environment fluctuates too far either side of the required state. There must then be some form of mechanism which comes into operation in order to return the conditions to normal. Such a system which automatically brings about a correction, regardless of which side of the optimum the change has occurred, is called a ***negative feedback*** system.

How the regulation of body temperature illustrates negative feedback

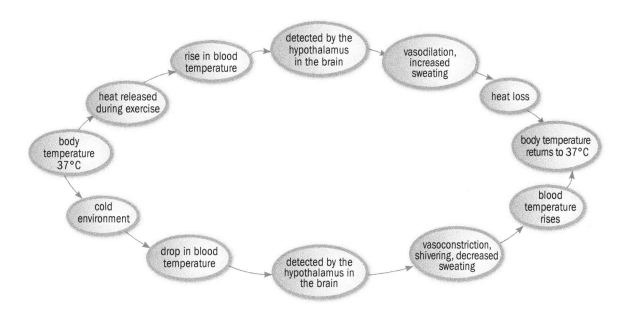

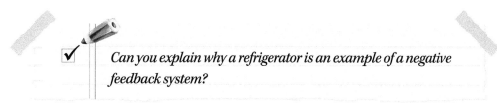

✔ *Can you explain why a refrigerator is an example of a negative feedback system?*

 Coordination and response

The brain and nervous system

The various organs of the body must work in coordination if an organism is to survive in its environment. To achieve this, the body has a number of ***receptors*** which pass information about the environment to a coordinating centre called the ***central nervous system*** (or ***CNS***).

The CNS (***brain*** and ***spinal cord***) receives the information (in the form of electrical ***impulses***), and then directs a ***response*** in the appropriate ***effectors*** (muscles or glands).

The most highly developed part of the CNS is the brain (Figure 4.12.)

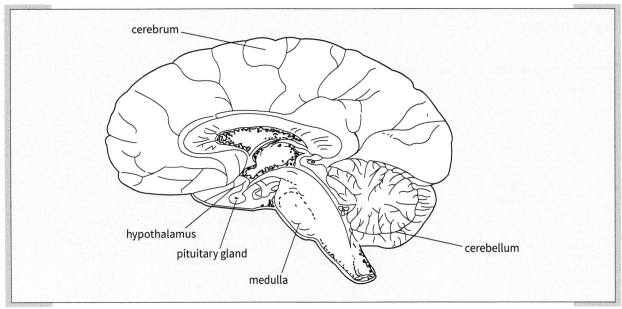

Figure 4.12 The human brain

The functions of the major parts of the brain

* The *cerebrum* is in the form of two matching halves – the *cerebral hemispheres* – and is responsible for the
  * *co-ordination* of the organs of the body
  * control of *voluntary* actions
  * reception of *sensation*.

At the very front of the *cerebrum* is the region responsible for memory and morals (the *higher mental activities*). At the back lies the region responsible for *sight*.

* The *cerebellum* is the region of *balance* and *instinct*.
* The *medulla* joins the brain to the spinal cord. It controls *unconscious* activities such as heartbeat, peristalsis and breathing.
* The *hypothalamus* lies under the cerebrum and is the part of the brain responsible for monitoring changes, particularly in the blood. It may be regarded as the 'homeostat' of the body.
* The *pituitary* gland.

Situated beneath the hypothalamus, this gland, which is made up only partly of nerve tissue, is sometimes called the 'master' gland, since it manufactures and releases into the blood chemicals (*hormones*) which control many glands and other organs throughout the body (such as those responsible for *growth*, e.g. of bones, and development (e.g., *sexual development*). It thus has a very important part to play in *co-ordination*. It regularly 'takes instruction' from the hypothalamus immediately above it.

The spinal cord

In the same way that a series of nerves (***cranial nerves***) serves the brain, impulses are relayed to and conducted from the spinal cord by nerves called ***spinal*** nerves. Spinal nerves are connected with receptors and effectors in parts of the body other than the head.

In emergency situations, the spinal cord can receive and transmit impulses to bring about rapid, often protective responses called ***reflex actions***. The central region of the spinal cord (the ***grey matter***) contains nerve cells (***relay neurones***) involved solely in this process. The outer region of the spinal cord (the ***white matter***) contains nerve cells involved in either supplying sensory information to the brain, or carrying impulses on their way to muscles which will contract under instruction from the brain (i.e. voluntary actions).

Nerves

A nerve is like a telephone cable; that is, it contains a large number of smaller 'wires' called ***neurones***. Each neurone is an individual nerve ***cell*** with its own cytoplasm, cell membrane and nucleus.

Neurones which conduct impulses from **sensory receptors** to the brain or spinal cord are called ***sensory*** neurones.

Neurones which then direct those impulses either to other parts of the brain or to other parts of the spinal cord are called ***relay*** neurones.

Neurones which conduct impulses from the brain or spinal cord to effectors (muscles or glands) are called ***motor*** (or ***effector***) neurones.

Neurones are ***insulated*** by a fatty (myelin) sheath. They are ***long***, they ***target*** the ***exact*** area to be affected and they conduct their impulses very ***quickly***. These features are vital if an action is to be taken very quickly to prevent damage as in a ***reflex action***.

NOTE

Never say 'nerve' when you mean 'neurone'.

The eye

The eye is one of the most important of the **receptors** providing us with information on ***dimensions, colours*** and ***distance away*** of objects in our environment. Its structural features are shown in Figure 4.13.

How the eye produces a focused image

1. ***Light rays*** from an object enter the ***transparent cornea***.
2. The cornea 'bends' (***refracts***) the light rays in towards one another.

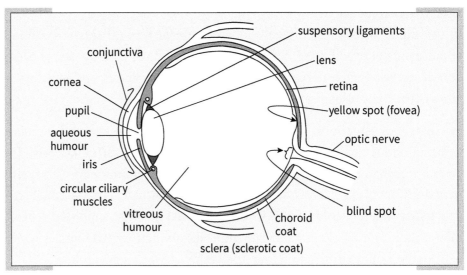

Figure 4.13 The eye

3. The light rays pass through the **aqueous humour** and **pupil**.
4. The **transparent, elastic lens** is altered in shape. It is made
   - fatter to **decrease** its **focal length**
   - thinner to **increase** focal length.
   This is called **accommodation**.
5. The relatively small amount of refraction now produced by the lens brings the rays to **focus** on the **retina**.
6. The retina contains **light – sensitive cells** (**rods**, which work well when light intensity is low, and **cones**, which give sharper definition and detect colour). These cells are the **receptors** and are stimulated by the light of the image. They convert the light energy into electrical energy.
7. Electrical energy, in the form of an **impulse**, travels along the **optic nerve** to the brain.
8. The brain **decodes** the impulses to produce the sensation of sight.

Other important facts

1. The image of objects that we are looking **directly** at (i.e. those that are in the centre of our field of vision) falls on a very sensitive part of the retina – the **fovea** (or **yellow spot**). This region has far more cones than rods. Cones provide a picture with greater detail as well as one that is in better colour.

2. There are **no** rods or cones at the point where the retina is joined to the optic nerve. Images formed on this part of the retina are not converted into impulses and relayed to the brain. This region is therefore called the **blind spot**. We have blind spots in both eyes, but are not usually aware of them. Each eye records a different part of our field of vision and one eye covers for the blind spot of the other.

You can demonstrate your blind spot as follows. With a marker pen, draw a cross (each line of the cross about 1 cm long) on a piece of paper. About 8 cm immediately to the right of the cross, draw a dot, also 1 cm in diameter. Cover your left eye with your hand, and position your head so that your right eye is about 15 cm away from the paper and directly in line with the cross. **Focus on the cross** *but you will also be able to see the dot, even though you are not looking straight at it. Keep looking at the cross, and keeping your left eye covered, now move your head slowly away from the paper (or the paper slowly away from your head). After a few centimetres, you will notice that the dot disappears, but reappears as you continue to increase the distance. The dot disappears as its image falls directly onto the blind spot in your right eye.*

Accommodation

The ability to change the shape and focal length of the lens to focus on objects at different distances is called **accommodation**. This ability depends on:

1. the **elasticity** of the lens
2. the existence of **ciliary** muscles, which are used to alter the shape of the lens
3. the **suspensory ligaments**, which transfer the effect of the ciliary muscles to the lens.

When viewing a near object:

1. The (circular) **ciliary muscles contract**, reducing their circumference.*
2. They reduce the pull on the (elastic) **suspensory ligaments**.
3. With less force on the **lens**, its elasticity allows it to become wider ('bulge') – **decreasing** its **focal length**.
4. Rays from the near object produce a focused image on the retina.

When viewing a distant object:

1. The (circular) ciliary muscles **relax**, increasing their circumference.*
2. The suspensory ligaments are **pulled tight**.
3. The lens is stretched to become longer and thinner – **increasing** its focal length.
4. Rays from the distant object are brought to focus on the retina.

NOTE

*The pressure of the vitreous humour stretches the ciliary muscles as they relax, and causes them to pull on the suspensory ligaments.

NOTE

As people age, the lenses in their eyes lose their elasticity.
This makes accommodation increasingly difficult, and they may require spectacles to view either near or distant objects – or both.

The value of having two eyes

Apart from overcoming the effect of the blind spot, two eyes view the same picture from two slightly different positions. This provides vision in **three dimensions**, the ability to **judge distance** (and therefore speed), and offers animals a chance of survival even if one eye is damaged.

The pupil (or iris) reflex

Bright light could seriously damage the delicate light-sensitive cells of the retina. The intensity of light falling on the retina is therefore controlled by the **iris**. It has an **antagonistic*** arrangement of **circular** and **radial** muscles as shown in Figure 4.14.

In bright light:

* ✳ Light-sensitive cells in the retina detect the light intensity.
* ✳ Impulses are sent along a nerve cell in the optic (**a sensory**) nerve to the brain.
* ✳ The brain returns impulses along a nerve cell in the **motor** nerve to the circular muscles of the iris.
* ✳ The circular iris muscles **contract** while the radial iris muscles **relax**.
* ✳ The diameter of the pupil, the hole in the centre, **decreases**, allowing less light to enter the eye, decreasing the risk of damage to the retina.

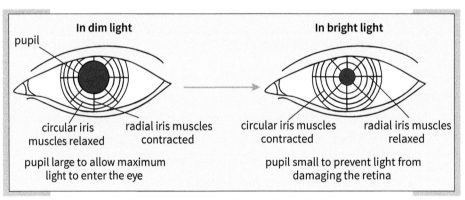

Figure 4.14 Antagonistic muscles in the iris

In dim light, the reverse of the above process occurs. The radial iris muscles contract and the circular iris muscles relax, increasing the diameter of the pupil allowing more light to enter the eye.

 You can demonstrate your own iris reflex by looking in a mirror, then turning on a lamp, such as a bench lamp, directed at your face. (A bulb of low intensity is suitable and avoids any risk of damage to your sight.)

NOTE

Although often referred to as the pupil reflex, this is really the iris reflex, since the iris contains the muscles. The pupil is simply a space.

NOTE

*Muscles can do their work only when they are **contracting**. Thus if an action is brought about by the contraction of one muscle, another muscle must be present to bring about the opposite effect. When one of this pair of muscles contracts, the other one **relaxes**. The two muscles together are referred to as an **antagonistic pair** of muscles.

In the example of the iris reflex, the brain was the part of the CNS involved, and the reflex action is thus called a **cranial** reflex.

When the spinal cord, alone, directs the response, then the action is described as a **spinal reflex** (e.g., when we rapidly withdraw our finger from a hot object).

The sequence of events in this spinal reflex is as follows (for named structural features see Figure 4.15):

1. A **stimulus** (the heat from the object) is received by the **sensory receptor** (in the finger).
2. An **impulse** is generated and carried along a **sensory neurone**.
3. The sensory neurone becomes part of a **spinal nerve**.
4. Impulses arrive at the nerve endings of the sensory neurone in the **grey matter** of the **spinal cord**.
5. The nerve endings release a **chemical** which diffuses across a gap – the **synapse** – between the sensory neurone and the nerve endings of a relay neurone. The chemical stimulates the **relay neurone** to produce an impulse.
6. Another synapse links the relay neurone with a **motor neurone**.
7. The impulse travels away from the spinal cord along the ventral root.

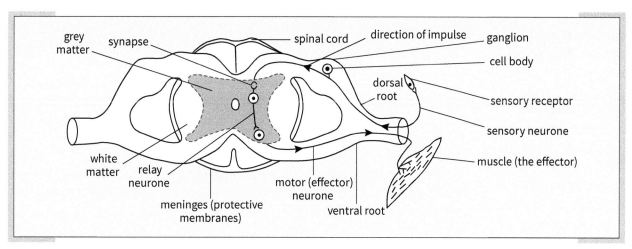

Figure 4.15 The reflex arc

8. The nerve endings of the motor neurone are applied to the **effector** (the **biceps** muscle in this case).
9. A **response** is produced (as the biceps muscle **contracts** to lift the hand clear of the stimulus).

Hormones

A **hormone** is *a chemical substance, produced by a gland and carried by the blood, which alters the activity of one or more specific target organs and is then destroyed by the liver.*

NOTE

Special cells in the islets of Langerhans in the pancreas produce a hormone – the rest of the organ produces *digestive juice*, which contains enzymes *not* hormones.

Hormones must be relatively **small, soluble**, easily **diffusible** chemical molecules, so that they can pass quickly from the cells that make them into (and later out of) blood capillaries. Blood then carries them to the organs on which they have their effect (the **target** organs).

Since the glands that produce hormones pass them directly into the blood, they have no ducts (small tubes to carry the hormones away) and are thus called **ductless** glands. The **adrenal** glands and the **pancreas** are examples of ductless glands.

The adrenal glands and the islets of the pancreas are examples of ductless glands.

NOTE

*Such emergencies would include the moments before the start of a competitive event (including an examination!), when being chased by an angry dog, or during a heated argument. Other effects of adrenaline, such as increasing blood pressure, diverting blood away from the intestines and towards the muscles about to be used, and increasing air flow to the lungs all help to make the body work more efficiently to meet the emergency.

gland	where situated	hormone produced	target organ	effect of hormone
adrenals	above the kidneys	*adrenaline* (the 'fight, fright and flight' hormone)	liver	turns glycogen into glucose to boost blood sugar level in emergencies*
			heart	heart beats faster – more oxygen to brain and muscles
			voluntary muscles	tire less easily
islets of Langerhans	in the pancreas	*insulin*	liver and muscles	promotes the uptake of glucose by cells and the conversion of glucose to glycogen for storage

Diabetes

If a person's islet cells produce insufficient insulin, then the level of **glucose in their blood will rise. Glucose** will be present in their **urine**, and the increased concentration of their blood plasma will draw water from their cells by osmosis, making them thirsty and tired, and causing them to urinate more frequently.

If insulin production is not seriously reduced, it may be possible to treat the condition by restricting the person's intake of carbohydrate. In **more extreme cases**, however, the treatment will include regular **injections** of insulin. The carbohydrate intake must then be regulated to match the amount of insulin injected.

 Support, movement and locomotion

Support refers to the skeleton and its role in holding the body structure clear of the ground and giving it shape.

Movement refers to the change in position of one part of the body in relation to another part.

Locomotion is the movement on the entire body from one place to another.

In animals, movement and locomotion could not occur without the **contraction** of **muscles**. Muscles provide the necessary **force**, and the bones of the **skeleton** to which the muscles are attached operate as **levers**.

The arrangement of bones in a limb is illustrated by the human arm (a mammalian fore-limb) in Figure 4.16.

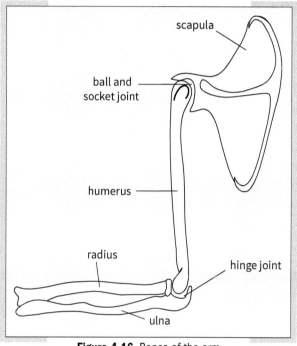

Figure 4.16 Bones of the arm

Although bones may be strongly fused together to provide protection (as in the skull), it is normal for them to be able to move freely on one another in order to permit movement. The **two** main types of joint which allow this movement are seen in the arm:

1. the **ball and socket joint** at the shoulder which allows free moment in **many planes** (though not quite 'all-round' movement)
2. the **hinge joint** at the elbow which allows movement in **one plane only**.

How muscles move bones at a joint

Muscles work in the following way (Structures involved are shown in Figure 4.17.):

* They can **pull** but never push.
* They pull **only** when they **contract**.
* When they contract, they **decrease** in length.
* When returning to their original length, they **relax** (not 'expand').
* They are attached to bones by **tendons** which do not stretch. They are arranged in **antagonistic pairs**, which apply their force either side of the bone they are required to move.
* One muscle of the pair (the **flexor**) **contracts** to bend the limb at the joint. As it does so, the other muscle in the pair (the **extensor**) **relaxes**.
* The **extensor** contracts to straighten the limb at the joint, and as it does so, the flexor relaxes. The arrangement of the antagonistic muscles at the hinge joint of the elbow are shown and described below.

NOTE

The muscles of the upper arm are the biceps and triceps. In the singular, both words have an 's' at the end, since biceps means 'two-heads' – referring to the two tendons at the top that fix it to the scapula at their lower ends, the biceps is fixed to the radius and the triceps to the ulna.

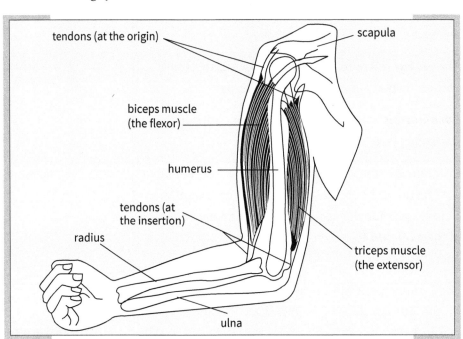

Figure 4.17 The muscles of the upper arm (showing the antagonistic arrangement)

How many other pairs of antagonistic muscles can you think of? Can you name a muscle that is not one of an antagonistic pair?

* Learn the difference between **aerobic** and the two forms of **anaerobic** respiration.

* Know the difference between **breathing** and **respiration**.

* Understand the mechanism of **breathing**.

* Know the features of a respiratory gas exchange surface, and the structure and function of an **alveolus** in particular.

* Learn the difference between the muscles involved in the iris reflex (the circular and radial iris muscles), and those involved in accommodation (the ciliary muscles).

* Understand what is meant by 'negative feedback', and be able to describe an example.

* Be able to define **homeostasis** and understand the terms **vasoconstriction** and **vasodilation**.

* Learn the structures and the sequence in which they are involved in a reflex arc.

* Make sure that you don't confuse hormones with enzymes.

* Know that muscles **contract** and **relax** (never 'expand'), they do work **only** when they are contracting and they **pull** (never 'push').

Exam-style questions for you to try

1. Which substance is filtered from the blood by the kidneys but does not appear in the urine of a healthy person?

   A. amino acids

   B. glucose

   C. toxins

   D. urea

2. What happens during expiration?

   A. The (external) intercostal muscles contract and the diaphragm flattens.

   B. The (external) intercostal muscles contract and the diaphragm relaxes.

   C. The (external) intercostal muscles relax and the diaphragm contracts.

   D. The (external) intercostal muscles relax and the diaphragm domes upwards.

3. Where does the process of accommodation occur in the eye shown in Figure 4.18?

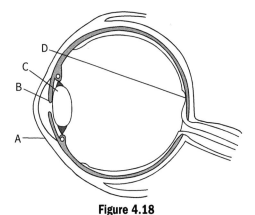

Figure 4.18

4. Which is the effector in the iris ('pupil') reflex?

   A. a motor neurone

   B. a sensory neurone

   C. the iris muscles

   D. the yellow spot (fovea)

5. Where is insulin made and what is its target organ?

	where made	target organ
A	Liver	Kidney
B	Kidney	Pancreas
C	Pancreas	Kidney
D	Pancreas	Liver

6. What describes how muscles work?

   A. they pull bones when they contract

   B. they push bones when they contract

   C. they pull bones when they relax

   D. they push bones when they relax

7. Figure 4.19 shows some structures in a section through human skin.

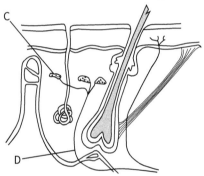

Figure 4.19

(a) The body is able to maintain its internal environment within narrow limits. State the term for this process.

.... [1]

(b) Structures C and D, in Figure 4.19, are involved in the process of temperature regulation. Identify structures C and D and state the part they play in the process.

C ....

part played ....

....

D ....

part played ....

.... [4]

(c) The consumption of alcohol causes the muscles in artery walls to relax.

Taking this into consideration, suggest why people who work in environmental temperatures below 5°C might be advised not to drink alcohol before or during work.

....

....

....

.... [3]

8. **(a)** Define the term *hormone*.

....

....

....

....

.... [4]

(b) Describe how insulin is involved in maintaining constant conditions within the body.

....

....

....

....

....

....

....

.... [6]

9. Figure 4.20 shows the pressure changes in a person's lungs during one complete breath out and in.

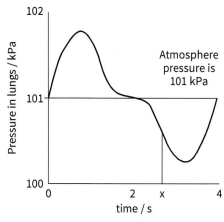

Figure 4.20

(a) Calculate the breathing rate of the person in breaths per minute

.... [1]

(b) Describe, and explain with reference to the muscles involved, what is happening at time X on the graph.

....

....

....

....

....

....

....

....

....

.... [8]

10. Figure 4.21 shows a person's rate of urine production in the 180 minutes after taking a drink of water.

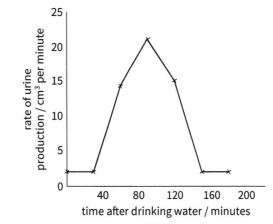

Figure 4.21

(a) State where most water is absorbed into the blood

.... [1]

(b) Using the graph, **(i)** estimate the length of time, after taking the drink, before excess water starts to be expelled from the blood ....

(ii) calculate the rate of urine production after 108 minutes.

.... [2]

(c) Explain how this graph would differ on a very hot day.

....

....

....

....

....

....

.... [5]

CHAPTER 5 Drugs, Microorganisms and the Environment

This chapter considers topics that are not centered on the biology of the plant or the human being, and take a wider view of life. There is a description of drug abuse and of biotechnology, followed by a section that covers topics that are, for the most part, more ecologically based, such as feeding relationships, natural cycles and how the human animal affects the environment in which it lives.

The use and abuse of drugs

Hormones are chemicals manufactured *by*, and *within*, a living organism, which have a specific effect on that organism's metabolism.

Chemicals, not made by the organism, may be introduced into the body of the organism for a specific effect. Such chemicals are called drugs.

A **drug** is *an externally administered substance which modifies or affects chemical reactions in the body.*

Drugs may be used for *beneficial* effects:

* *For pain relief* (e.g., aspirin, paracetamol and morphine).

* For *treatment of disease*. Diseases caused by *bacteria*, such as *syphilis*, are treated with drugs called *antibiotics*, of which a well-known example is *penicillin*.

* Drugs are also used for their *mood-influencing* effects. This can be useful for treating patients with emotional disorders such as depression.

Drug abuse

If a drug is taken simply for enjoyment (i.e. it is used as a 'recreational' drug), and often therefore in high dosage, it can lead to *addiction*.

Heroin is a drug which is abused in this way. It is a *powerful depressant*. Depressants are drugs that affect the central nervous system slowing (or 'depressing') the rate at which impulses are conducted and removing all feelings of anxiety and creating a feeling of extreme well-being. Heroin is a drug to which the body shows *tolerance*, as a result of which progressively *increased* dosages are required in order to give the same effect.

The person using the drug ('user') may end up in a state of **dependence** in which they cannot face life without the drug. The user begins to crave the drug, and if unable to obtain further supplies, suffers severe **withdrawal symptoms** which include diarrhoea, vomiting, muscular pain, shaking and hallucination. These are signs that abuse of the drug has led to addiction.

Addiction can lead the user into a life of **crime** in order to obtain money and/or regular supplies of the drug. Heroin is a drug normally taken by injection into a vein. If several addicts use the same unsterilised needles, they are at a high risk of contracting blood-borne diseases such as **hepatitis** and **AIDS**.

Alcohol is a more widely available and more widely used drug. It is generally regarded as a more 'socially acceptable' drug by many societies, but its effects are as follows:

* It is a **depressant**, creating a feeling of well-being.
* It **slows reaction times** (increasing the risk of accident).
* When consumed in **excessive** quantities, it leads to **loss of self-control**. Many people under the influence of alcohol behave in a way of which they would be ashamed of when sober.
* It also leads to **liver damage** ('cirrhosis') which can eventually prove fatal.

Like heroin, alcohol is a drug of addiction, and thus, to prevent withdrawal symptoms (which are not as severe as those for heroin), considerable amounts of money are spent to satisfy the cravings. Often a person's **family suffers**, not only from a lack of financial support, but also from **physical violence** which often accompanies alcoholism.

Nicotine is the drug of addiction present in cigarette smoke. A person suffers (relatively) mild withdrawal symptoms if the craving is not satisfied. Nicotine has the following effects:

* It is a **poison** which **increases heart rate** and **blood pressure**.
* It may cause **blood clotting** increasing the risk of **thrombosis** (which if in the coronary artery of the heart will result in a heart 'attack').

Other harmful components of cigarette smoke:

* **Tar** forms a layer over the walls of the alveoli, restricting gaseous exchange. It is also a **carcinogen** (i.e. a cancer producer) and prolonged exposure to it may lead to **lung cancer**.
* **Carbon monoxide** is taken up, permanently, by **haemoglobin** in preference to oxygen (forming carboxyhaemoglobin). It thus greatly **reduces** the ability of the **blood** to carry **oxygen** to the extremities

(fingers and toes), which can be especially affected, as can those parts that require a lot of oxygen to keep working – such as the heart.

* *Irritant chemicals* and *particles* in smoke cause cells lining the bronchi and bronchioles to increase their production of *mucus*. These chemicals also *destroy the cilia* lining the trachea. Cilia sweep away the dirt in a 'moving carpet' of mucus and carry it to the throat for swallowing. The build-up of mucus is relieved only by continual coughing (smoker's cough). Persistent coughing eventually damages the walls of the alveoli (*emphysema*).

* A pregnant woman who smokes also *risks the health of her baby*. *Less oxygen* reaches the baby as a result of the effects of carbon monoxide, and *nicotine* can pass from mother's to baby's blood. Babies born to mothers who smoke during pregnancy have been shown to be *underweight*, perhaps less intelligent, and there is a greater risk of *miscarriage*.

* *Passive smoking*. Evidence now exists that breathing the smoke from other people can be harmful, and cigarette smoke is certainly an *irritant* to the eyes and leaves a lingering smell in clothes. Smoking is therefore increasingly becoming a *socially unacceptable habit*.

NOTE

In total, there are over 4000 different chemicals in smoke, of which at least 50 are known to cause cancer.

Diseases associated with smoking

Other than the risk of heart disease mentioned above, smoking greatly increases the chances of suffering from the following diseases:

1. *Chronic bronchitis*: Bronchitis is an inflammation of the airways ('chronic' means extending over a long period of time). It leads to an overproduction of mucus which tends to block the bronchi and bronchioles, making breathing difficult, and decreasing the efficiency of the gaseous exchange process. Less oxygen reaches the blood, with consequent effects on organs such as the heart muscle, the brain and the extremities. It also causes a distressing cough.

2. *Emphysema*: Emphysema is a condition often associated with chronic bronchitis. The walls of the alveoli become stretched and lose their elasticity. They do not empty properly creating a build-up of carbon dioxide in the lungs. The patient suffers from breathlessness, and decreased efficiency of heart, brain, etc., through too much carbon dioxide (and insufficient oxygen) in the blood.

3. *Lung cancer*: Cells in the lungs begin to divide uncontrollably, forming thickened tissues through which gases cannot pass, and which may block airways. Unless treated early, it is likely to be a fatal condition.

Microorganisms and biotechnology

All organisms are collections of chemical molecules which, when working together, show what are recognised as the 'characteristics of life' (respiration, reproduction, excretion, nutrition, sensitivity, growth, movement and a cellular structure). Microorganisms are organisms which are studied only with the aid of a microscope. Often, they are made up of one cell only (i.e. **unicellular**).

Viruses

Viruses are the simplest of all forms of life – so simple, in fact, that biologists do not regard them as truly living. They have the following main characteristics:

1. They are less than 300 nm in size – around 50 times smaller than a bacterium (1 nm or nanometre, is one thousand millionth of a metre). They can be seen only with an **electron microscope**.
2. They contain **nucleic acid** (DNA or RNA*).
3. The nucleic acid is surrounded by a **coat** of **protein** (two such coats in the case of HIV – known as the capsid).
4. They can **reproduce only inside living** ('host') **cells**.
5. Since they are **parasites**, they **cause disease** (i.e. they are **pathogenic**). Examples of diseases caused by viruses are influenza, measles and AIDS.
6. Viruses are **not affected by antibiotics**.

Structural features of a virus are shown in Figure 5.1.

 NOTE

*Like DNA, RNA is a nucleic acid. It is important in the process by which proteins are made in cells of higher organisms.

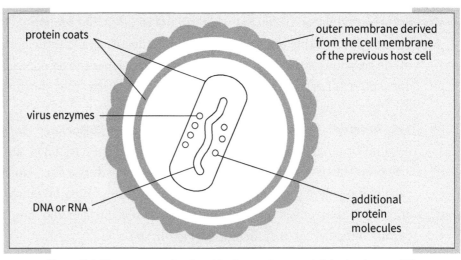

Figure 5.1 The structure of a virus (the human immunodeficiency virus, or HIV, has RNA as its nucleic acid)

Bacteria

Bacteria are the simplest of the truly living organisms. They have the following characteristics:

1. They have a size in the range of 0.5–5 μm.
2. They are **unicellular** (made of one cell only).
3. They have **no true nucleus** (their DNA lies 'loose' in the cytoplasm).
4. They have a **cell wall**.
5. They may be **(pathogenic) parasites** or they may be **saprotrophs** – feeding on dead organic matter **causing** it to decay. Some may be involved in **nitrogen fixation** (see the nitrogen cycle).
6. They are killed by **antibiotics**.

Structural features of a bacterium are shown in Figure 5.2.

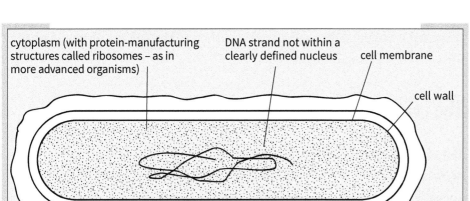

cytoplasm (with protein-manufacturing structures called ribosomes – as in more advanced organisms)

DNA strand not within a clearly defined nucleus

cell membrane

cell wall

1 μm

capsule (not always present)

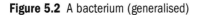

Figure 5.2 A bacterium (generalised)

Fungi

These are much larger organisms and usually visible to the naked eye. They have the following characteristics:

1. They have **no chlorophyll**, and thus have heterotrophic nutrition (i.e. they digest large molecules with enzymes and absorb the soluble products). They are thus **parasites** or **saprotrophs**.
2. They have a 'cell' wall made of **chitin**.
3. They are usually made of a large number of tubular threads (**hyphae**) intertwined to form a **mycelium**.
4. Hyphae are not divided into individual cells. The lining of **cytoplasm has many nuclei** and the central space in the hyphae is a **vacuole** full of (vacuolar) **sap**.
5. If they store carbohydrate, they **store glycogen**.
6. They reproduce by producing **spores**.

Drugs, Microorganisms and the Environment 113

The role of microorganisms in decomposition

When microorganisms such as bacteria and fungi feed as **saprotrophs**, they use **external digestion**. They bring about decomposition of dead organic matter by **releasing enzymes** onto their dead organic substrate ('food'). These enzymes are:

* **protease**, which digests proteins to amino acids (amino acids are then further broken down to **ammonium ions**)
* **amylase**, which digests starch to simple sugars
* **lipase**, which digests fats to fatty acids and glycerol.

Some of the end products are absorbed by the microorganisms for use in their own metabolism. E.g., amino acids for building up proteins during growth; sugars for energy release during respiration – with CO_2 and H_2O as waste products; fats for energy storage. Gradually, the dead matter is broken down, releasing its mineral ions which are returned to the soil for recycling as they are taken up for use by plants.

The roles of bacteria and fungi in food production

Bacteria and yoghurt

Milk is heated to 90°C, and then cooled to between 40°C and 45°C. The correct species of bacterium (e.g., **Lactobacillus**) is added and the milk is kept at this temperature for 24–36 hours. Over this time, the bacteria convert milk sugar into **lactic acid** by **anaerobic respiration**. The acid **curdles** the milk to produce the characteristic texture and sharp flavour of yoghurt.

Bacteria and cheese

Milk, is warmed to 40°C, inoculated with **bacteria** (**Streptococcus**) and mixed with **rennin**, an enzyme found in the stomachs of young mammals to speed up the curdling of milk. Lactic acid produced by the bacteria creates the correct pH for the rennin to work. The milk curdles (or 'clots'). The solid part (the **curd**) is separated from the liquid (the **whey**). The curd is pressed and moulded and left to mature (or ripen). Sometimes, further bacteria are added to provide flavour, e.g., from copper wires which are drawn through the dried curd.

Yeast and alcohol

Yeast is a **fungus**. It is added to a sugar solution to make alcohol. E.g., yeast is added to fruit sugar such as from grapes to make wine; yeast is added to maltose obtained from barley to make beer. The yeast is allowed to **ferment** the sugar at a **controlled temperature** – the optimum for the growth of yeast (around 20°C) in a vessel (the **fermenter**). By **anaerobic respiration** the yeast converts the sugar to **alcohol** with **carbon dioxide** evolved as a waste product. As the concentration of alcohol rises, it eventually kills the yeast which must then be filtered from the liquor to produce a yeast-free alcoholic drink. Drinks with a higher alcoholic content such as spirits are produced by **distillation** of the original alcoholic drink (brandy is distilled wine).

Yeast and bread

A process similar to the one described above occurs in bread-making. This time, though, flour and water are used to make a dough, to which yeast and a little sugar are added. Although alcohol is produced by the anaerobic respiration of the yeast, it is the **carbon dioxide** which is now important. The mixture is left in a **warm** place for around half an hour (depending on temperature) for the dough to 'prove'. The carbon dioxide gas causes the dough to rise, giving it a light texture. The dough is then **baked** at **high temperature** in an oven. The high temperature cooks the bread and evaporates the alcohol produced during fermentation and kills the yeast.

Industrial biotechnology

Biotechnology is used in many industrial processes, e.g., in the manufacture of **antibiotics** and of **single-cell protein (SCP)**. Since large quantities of end product are required, the microorganisms involved are grown in very large containers called **fermenters**. *A maximum rate of growth* of the microorganism within the fermenter can be achieved by careful control of

* the **temperature**
* the type and concentration of **substrate** (i.e. the substance on which the microorganism works)
* the **oxygen availability**.

Thus, fermenters are not affected by climate, soil type or, in temperate regions, time of year, though they must be kept **sterile** to prevent the growth of unwanted species of microorganism which might contaminate the end product.

The manufacture of the antibiotic penicillin

Pathogenic (disease-causing) bacteria are known to be killed by certain chemicals (**antibiotics**) released by other microorganisms – especially fungi.

NOTE

Although the word *litre* is in common use, it is considered better to use the term 'cubic decimetre' which is abbreviated to dm³.

The ***mould fungus*** *Penicillium*, which grows naturally on stale bread, is first cultured on a sterile medium in a laboratory.

The fungus is then introduced into a fermenter (Figure 5.3) for commercial production. The fermenter (up to 100 000 dm³ in volume) contains a suitable sterile medium on which the fungus can grow. One medium used is 'corn-steep liquor' – a waste product from the milling of maize. It provides amino acids for growth and carbohydrates for respiration and therefore energy.

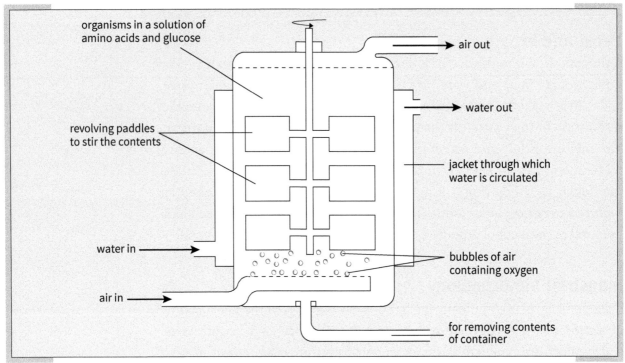

Figure 5.3 A fermenter

After an appropriate period of time (when the rate of fungal growth becomes limited by the amount of food available), the contents of the fermenter are removed and filtered. The liquid part contains the antibiotic (in this case, ***penicillin***), which is ***separated*** and ***purified***, while the rest of the material may be dried and used as cattle feed.

Bearing in mind the lifestyle of bacteria and fungi, why do you think it is advantageous for fungi to produce chemicals that have the ability to kill bacteria?

Single-cell protein production

Since bacteria and fungi contain cytoplasm, and since a major constituent of cytoplasm is **protein**, it follows that large-scale production of these microorganisms involves the large-scale production of protein. The process is carried out in a fermenter and the microorganisms thus grown can be harvested and used as a protein source. Such protein is known as SCP (single-cell protein). If the microorganisms concerned are fungi, then, more accurately, the protein is known as **mycoprotein**.

Many microorganisms will grow successfully on industrial waste materials as a substrate, e.g., waste from oil refining, waste from sugar refining (molasses), whey from cheese manufacture, and straw.

NOTE

Some forms of mycoprotein are sold as a meat substitute as it can have a similar texture to meat. It has the advantage of being free from fat and cholesterol, and is a suitable alternative to meat for vegetarians.

 # The relationships of organisms with each other and the environment

Energy flow

The source of energy for all life on the planet is **the Sun**. Living organisms use that energy for their activities, and so long as the Sun continues to shine life can continue.

The **heat energy** from the Sun is used by organisms such as 'cold-blooded' animals to keep their bodies warm. The Sun also supplies the **light energy** which is locked away by plants during **photosynthesis** to form **chemical energy** in food molecules. If those plants are eaten by animals, which may themselves be eaten by other animals, the energy is passed on again. In this way, the sun's energy **enters** and then **flows** through biological (eco)systems, and is gradually **lost** to the environment as it passes from one organism to the next. It is **never recycled**.

Food chains and food webs

Starting with the plant that locks the light energy away as it photo-synthesises, the energy then passes through successive organisms which make up a particular **food chain**.

A food chain is a chart showing the flow of energy (food) from one organism to the next beginning with a producer.

Below is an example of a food chain in a lake:

green algae   →   mosquito larvae   →   small fish   →   heron

(Example: *Anopheles*)   (Example: small *Tilapia*)

Algae are unicellular organisms which contain chlorophyll and photosynthesise.

In any one habitat, such as a lake, pond or mangrove swamp, there will be many organisms living together forming an ***ecosystem***. The food chains involving all of these organisms will be interconnected.

A **food web**, therefore, is a *series of interlinked food chains involving organisms within one ecosystem.*

All food chains, and thus all food webs, begin with a photosynthesising organism, the ***producer***. All those organisms that rely on energy supplied by the producer are known as ***consumers***.

When all organisms in a food chain/web die, they are decomposed by saprotrophic organisms – usually bacteria and fungi.

key term	transpiration slowed down by	example
producer	an organism that makes its own organic nutrients using energy from sunlight through photosynthesis	green algae, plants
consumer	an organism that gets its energy by feeding on other organisms	mosquito larvae, small fish, heron
herbivore (or primary consumer)	an animal that obtains its energy by eating plants.	mosquito larvae
secondary consumers	consumers that feed directly on the herbivore	small fish
tertiary consumers	consumers that feed directly on the secondary consumer	heron
carnivore	an animal that obtains its energy by eating other animals	small fish, heron
decomposer	an organism that obtains its energy from dead or waste organic matter	bacteria, fungi

✔ *Try to construct three food chains for different environments. Each food chain should begin with a producer and have at least three links.*

Energy loss along a food chain

Some of the energy locked away by producers (plants) is **released** by the producer itself through the process of **respiration**. Some of the energy is **used** by the producer, e.g., for **cell division**, **growth** and **reproduction**. A lot of the energy is still present when the plant dies, and is then available to decomposers. Only some of it (around 10%) is passed on to the herbivores that eat the plants. This is shown in Figure 5.4.

Herbivores then **release the energy** by respiration, and use it for

* growth
* movement (muscle contraction)
* to generate electrical nerve impulses
* for active transport of chemicals through cell membranes
* as heat, to maintain body temperature.

Much of the energy is still present in the faeces and some in the nitrogenous waste. This is available to decomposers. Not all herbivores are eaten; thus, the amount of energy left within herbivores to be passed on to carnivores is small – 20% (only 2% of the original amount in the producer).

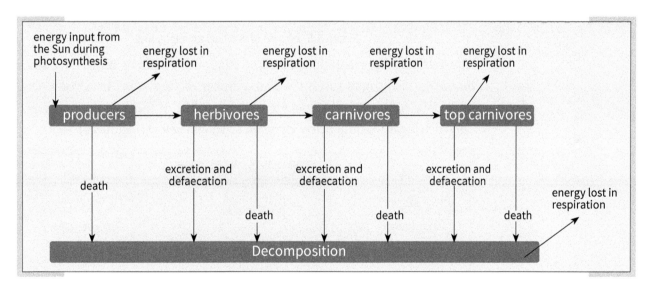

Figure 5.4 Energy flow in an ecosystem

The longer the food chain, the less energy is available to the top carnivore at the end of the chain. **Short** food chains are therefore much more energy efficient than long ones. In order to supply enough energy in food to maintain an ever-increasing world population, it must be realised that far less energy is lost when humans eat green plants than when crop plants are fed to animals which are then eaten by humans.

Pyramids of numbers and biomass

Producers (plants) need to produce enough food – and therefore lock away enough energy – for their own metabolic processes. They must also provide enough food (and therefore energy) for the herbivores that eat them, and leave enough surviving individuals to reproduce the next generation. Therefore, we would expect there to be **a larger number of producers (plants) than primary consumers (herbivores)**. For the same reasons, we would expect there to be more primary consumers than secondary consumers, and so on. These decreasing numbers along a food web can be represented in the form of a **pyramid of numbers** as shown below (Figure 5.5).

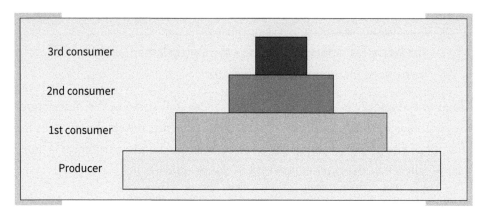

Figure 5.5 Pyramid of numbers for a food web

However, this representation of feeding relationships can be misleading, since **one large** plant may sustain a large number of very small herbivores. One secondary consumer may sustain a large number of third order consumers. This then leads to a 'top heavy' pyramid as shown below (Figure 5.6).

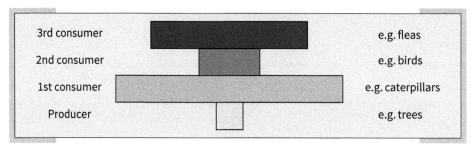

Figure 5.6 'Top heavy' pyramid of numbers for a particular food chain

A **pyramid of biomass** is a pyramid constructed using the **dry mass** of organisms at each trophic level in a food chain (or food web). It produces pyramids of a more familiar shape (as in Figure 5.5) and can be constructed by collecting data from population estimates in any particular habitat. Dry mass is the mass of an organism, minus the mass of its water content.

Biomass is the total dry mass of a population, i.e. the theoretical mass of chemicals other than water in the organisms under consideration (water being liable to considerable variation).

The carbon cycle

When ***decomposition*** occurs, carbohydrates in the dead organic matter are used as the substrate for respiration by decomposers (bacteria and fungi). ***Carbon dioxide*** is released into the atmosphere, as it is in all cases of aerobic ***respiration***.

Combustion – the burning of fuels also ***releases carbon dioxide*** into the atmosphere. Many of these fuels are fossil fuels such as coal, gas and oil.

Photosynthesis – absorbs that carbon dioxide and converts it into carbohydrates (which may then be used to make fats or proteins) in a plant.

Animal nutrition involves the transfer of these carbon-containing molecules to animals. Animals and plants ***respire***, and eventually die and are decomposed, releasing the carbon dioxide back into the atmosphere, and so the cycle continues. Figure 5.7 shows how the processes in the carbon cycle are linked.

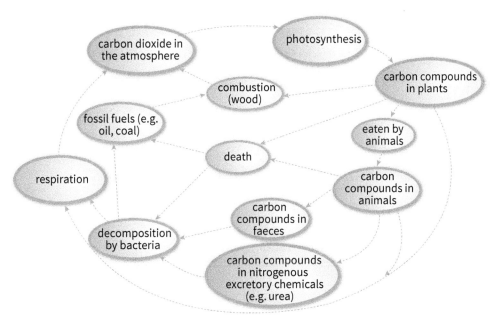

Figure 5.7 The carbon cycle

The nitrogen cycle

Decomposition includes the conversion by bacteria of ***proteins*** to ***amino acids***, and the conversion of amino acids and ***urea*** to ***ammonium ions***. This process usually takes place in the soil.

Ammonium ions contain ***nitrogen*** atoms, but before plants can absorb nitrogen from the soil, it must be in the form of ***nitrate*** ions.

Nitrifying bacteria convert ammonium ions first into ***nitrites***, and then into ***nitrates***.

Plants absorb the nitrates and use them, together with the carbohydrates made by photosynthesis, to make amino acids and then *proteins*.

Animals eat the protein in the plants and excrete, e.g., urea. Both plants and animals die and their decomposition releases ammonium ions again.

Atmospheric nitrogen (78% of the air) cannot be used either by plants or by animals in its gaseous form, but some bacteria (the **nitrogen-fixing bacteria**) can do so. These bacteria are found in **two forms**:

* those which live in swellings called *nodules* on the roots of peas, beans and other plants in this family (known as *leguminous* plants)
* those which live freely in the soil

Nitrogen fixation by these bacteria changes the atmospheric nitrogen, via ammonia, into *proteins*. The nitrogen becomes available to other organisms when these proteins later decompose.

Nitrogen fixation also occurs when *lightning* passes through the nitrogen in the air, converting it to *nitric acid*, which forms nitrates in the soil.

All the processes above are linked in the nitrogen cycle as shown in Figure 5.8.

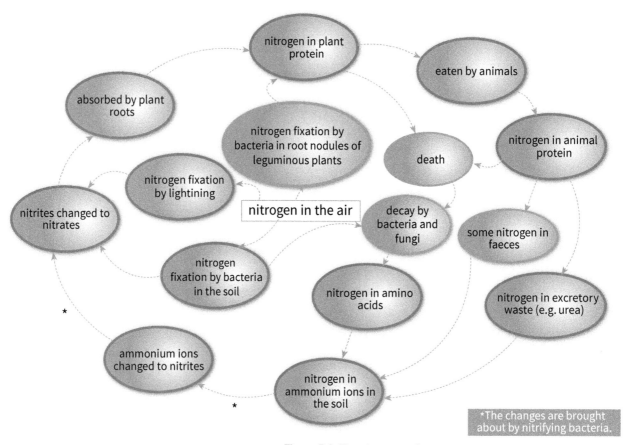

Figure 5.8 The nitrogen cycle

Parasitism

A **parasite** can be defined as *an organism which obtains its food from another, usually larger living organism ('host'); the host always suffers in the relationship.*

Pathogens (disease-causing organisms) are therefore parasites, one such pathogen being the unicellular organism *Plasmodium* which causes **malaria**.

The transmission of malaria

Malaria is a disease **caused** by a **single-celled microorganism** called **Plasmodium** that lives in red blood cells. It is carried from person to person (host to host) by the **female Anopheles mosquito**. The mosquito is thus described as the **vector** (i.e. carrier) of the microorganism. Usually at night, while the host is asleep, she injects her saliva into a (healthy) person before she starts to suck the blood which she needs for her developing eggs. The saliva contains a chemical to stop the blood from clotting. If the mosquito has recently taken blood from a person **infected** with malaria it may also contain the parasite *Plasmodium*. The parasite has now been transferred **from** the **blood** of one host, where it lives and develops, **to** the **blood** of a second host.

Control of malaria

Malaria can be controlled in three ways:

1. by controlling the mosquito vector
2. by avoiding mosquito bites
3. by treating the parasite in the blood.

Controlling the mosquito

* Cover water tanks with netting to stop mosquitoes laying their eggs in the water.
* Drain swamps and areas of stagnant water where mosquitoes lay their eggs.
* Introduce fish such as **Tilapia** into the swamps to feed on mosquito larvae.
* Cover the surface of the water with light oil. Larvae cannot then use the water film from which they hang as they breathe air from the atmosphere. The larvae therefore suffocate.
* Use insecticides or mosquito coils to kill adult mosquitoes inside buildings.

Avoiding mosquito bites

* Place nets over doors and windows.
* Wear clothes which cover wrists and ankles, especially in the evenings, when mosquitoes are most active.
* Use insect repellent sprays.
* Sleep under mosquito nets.

Protection against the parasite *Plasmodium*

* Take drugs regularly to kill the parasite if it enters the bloodstream (e.g., Paludrine, but the correct drug must be taken for the particular type of *Plasmodium* found in any particular region).
* Treat patients suffering from malaria with a higher dosage of anti-malarial drug, and isolate them to prevent spreading of the disease.

The effects of humans on the ecosystem

The human animal is as much part of the ecosystem in which it lives as any other organism in that ecosystem. But humans can be far more destructive than any other of their fellow organisms.

Deforestation

A great deal of natural woodland has been (and is being) destroyed for the following reasons:

* to harvest timber for building houses and making furniture
* to make way for motorways and industrial development
* to create agricultural land for the growth of crops and the rearing of cattle.

The dangers of deforestation

The loss of soil stability

1. The loss of humus in the soil – leaves from the trees fall to the ground where they decompose forming ***humus*** in the soil.

    Humus:

    a. provides a steady supply of ions
    b. acts as a sponge, soaking up and holding water in the soil
    c. helps to bind the soil together thus preventing soil erosion.

2. The loss of protection from excessive sun, wind and rain – trees form a ***canopy*** which keeps the powerful Sun's rays off more delicate organisms. The canopy also protects the soil from the force of tropical rainfall, and protects the soil as well as smaller plants and animals

from the full force of high winds. Tree **roots** also help to bind the soil. Removal of the trees therefore leads to soil **erosion** caused by wind and water, and soil carried into rivers may lead to **flooding** further downstream as it is deposited on the bed of the river as **silt**.

The effect on climate

Trees supply enormous quantities of water vapour to the atmosphere as a result of **transpiration**. Transpiration leads to the formation of clouds. Clouds are carried by the prevailing winds and eventually produce rain, usually in an area some distance away from where the vapour was released. Deforestation, therefore, can lead to distant regions receiving **reduced rainfall**. At its most extreme, relatively fertile areas can become **deserts**.

On a global scale, deforestation can reduce the amount of carbon dioxide taken in for photosynthesis. **The levels of carbon dioxide in the atmosphere rise**, acting as a 'thermal blanket' over the planet, preventing the natural escape of heat from our atmosphere (the **greenhouse effect**). This is believed to lead to **global warming** which may affect the distribution of plants and animals (and eventually melt the ice caps).

The effect on local human populations

Deforestation is usually motivated by financial gain. Those who benefit often live outside the country where the deforestation is occurring. Many local residents **lose their homes** and see their **culture destroyed** along with the trees. Many find it **difficult to adapt** to lifestyles which are geared to commercial success. These problems are being faced by people living in the Amazon Rain Forest of South America, which is one of the largest areas of deforestation in the world.

Pollution

Apart from the effects of deforestation, humans are also responsible for polluting the environment in a number of ways. These are discussed here.

The pollution of water by sewage

Large human settlements create a considerable amount of sewage. Tipping sewage directly into streams and rivers can have the following harmful effects:

* Sewage contains pathogenic organisms. If the water is used for human consumption, then diseases, such as **cholera**, can be spread.
* Very high levels of sewage contain very large numbers of **bacteria** which use up the oxygen in the water for their own respiration. This leaves insufficient oxygen for other forms of water life, so many organisms die.

* Smaller quantities of sewage release ions as it decomposes. These ions encourage rapid growth of water plants (*eutrophication*), which eventually die and decompose (see 'Water pollution by nitrogen-containing fertilisers').

Water pollution by inorganic waste

* ***Household detergents***, discharged into rivers along with sewage, often contain phosphates. These encourage the growth of small (photosynthesising) water organisms (green algae), leading to possible eutrophication.

* ***Industrial wastes*** such as those which contain **mercury** (e.g., from paper mills) and **copper** ('heavy metals') are highly toxic to all organisms. It is expensive to remove these wastes in a completely safe way, and thus they too may be discharged into rivers.

Polluted rivers discharge into **seas**. Polluted seas lead to contamination of producers in the sea's food chains. One small fish consumes many smaller contaminated food organisms. One large fish eats many smaller fish, and in this way, the amount of ***poison gradually increases*** in the organisms ***along the food chain***. When contaminated fish is used as food for humans, harmful levels of poison can be consumed.

Water pollution by nitrogen-containing fertilisers

The removal of trees and the loss to the soil of decaying organic matter (humus) encourage the use of artificial fertilisers to obtain the maximum crop yields. However, we have also seen that deforestation leads to flooding and water is washed from the loose soil into rivers. This water takes with it the dissolved fertilisers (***nitrates and ammonium salts***) and these encourage the growth of green algae and water plants in the rivers (eutrophication). The algae and plants can block rivers and prevent light from penetrating to lower depths. Eventually, the algae and plants die, and bacteria begin to decompose them. The bacteria respire aerobically, extracting large quantities of oxygen from the river water. A lack of oxygen prevents aquatic animals such as fish and insect larvae from respiring, so they, too, die.

Air pollution by greenhouse gases (carbon dioxide and methane)

The effect of a build-up of carbon dioxide has been discussed earlier under deforestation above. Carbon dioxide is also released during the burning of fossil

NOTE

The term 'eutrophication' refers **only** to the abundant growth of plant matter in natural bodies of water. The subsequent changes that occur as a result of this enhanced growth (such as depletion of oxygen) do **not** form part of eutrophication.

fuels; thus, factories and motor vehicles add to the problem of global warming. Carbon dioxide is not the only greenhouse gas. The intensive farming of food animals such as cows and sheep also contributes the greenhouse gas *methane*. A cow releases between 60 kg and 120 kg methane per year, and a sheep, 8 kg per year from their digestive systems.

NOTE

A human makes the modest contribution of 0.12 kg per year!

Air pollution by acidic gases (sulphur dioxide and oxides of nitrogen)

Sulphur dioxide and oxides of nitrogen (e.g., nitrogen dioxide) are gases which are released whenever *fossil fuels* are burnt. In industrial areas, the amounts of these gases released into the air can be high. Sulphur dioxide is a gas that is harmful to humans, and is linked to bronchitis and heart disease.

In the air, it dissolves in rain to fall to earth as a dilute solution of *sulphuric acid*. Nitrogen dioxide dissolves in rain to form *nitric acid*. Rain containing these dissolved gases is known as *acid rain*, which has the following effects:

* It kills the leaves of some species of plant (fe.g., wheat).

* It makes the water of lakes *acidic*. This acidic water now dissolves toxic chemicals (such as salts of aluminium) present in the mud of the lake and which are insoluble in neutral or alkaline solutions. Fish, e.g., are killed by aluminium.

Pollution due to insecticides

Insects cause considerable harm to the economy, either as pests on crops or as vectors of disease. They can be killed very effectively by *insecticides*, but insecticides may pollute the environment with the following harmful effects:

* *Useful* insects, such as those needed for *pollination*, may be killed as well.

* If the livers of animals are unable to break down the insecticide, it may be passed from animal to animal along food chains. Since animals at any trophic level may eat many animals from the trophic level immediately before it (which may have been insects affected by insecticide) animals at the end of a food chain can receive a very high, and perhaps very harmful, level of insecticide. E.g., some birds are known to have been made sterile.

* Agricultural pesticides can be washed into rivers, thus entering food chains in the water as well as on land.

The need for conservation

The threat of extinction

The removal of organisms from an environment at a faster rate than the organism can reproduce itself leads to **extinction** of the species. Widespread deforestation can therefore lead to extinction of plant species; uncontrolled fishing can lead to the extinction of species of fish.

Destruction of habitats, however it may occur, may also lead to the extinction of animal species which live amongst the plants, are protected by them and are linked to them through food chains.

Plants are the source of many valuable products such as drugs. **Aspirin** (for pain relief and treatment of circulatory disorders), **quinine** (for the treatment of malaria) and many other drugs were first obtained from plants. Deforestation could rob humans of the plant which might bring a **cure** for diseases such as AIDS.

Maintaining a continuous supply of commodities from trees

Timber, rubber and **oils** are commodities, or useful products, supplied by trees. Most trees that supply commodities grow very slowly: the product they supply may not be ready to harvest until many years after planting. A system of **sustainable management** must therefore be used, this means harvesting only the number of trees that can be replaced by planting.

Maintaining fish supplies

The oceans supply many communities with a large part of their food requirements. **Over-fishing** can reduce fish populations to a point where they are not able to maintain their numbers. Fishing **quotas** (legally enforced limits on the mass of fish that can be caught) make sure that stocks remain at sustainable levels, but they must be adhered to.

The conservation of other species

In order to maintain the wide variety (**biodiversity**) of living species on the planet, it is important to identify **threatened species** so that their needs can be addressed before it is too late. This work is carried out by WWF (the Worldwide Fund for Nature) and CITES (the Convention on International Trade in Endangered Species). Countries throughout the world must then support such organisations with legislation.

The importance of recycling materials

Pressure is taken off endangered species if countries encourage a policy of recycling.

* Many **car parts** and **drinks cans** are now made of recycled **metal**. This reduces the need for mining activity and consequently the effect that mining has on the environment. The burning of fossil fuels used to produce the heat needed to extract metals from their ores is also reduced.

* **Bottles** are made from recycled **glass**.

* **Paper** is also recycled, reducing the number of trees that need to be cut down for fibres that are used to make paper products.

* **Litter** is also reduced by recycling, making our environment a more pleasant place in which to live, but an ever-increasing component of everyday **litter** is **plastic**. Most **plastics are non-biodegradable**, which means that, though they may well be made of organic chemicals, they are not decomposed by bacteria or fungi. It is therefore important that they are recycled whenever possible. Another problem is the very high temperatures necessary to melt the plastic – as this tends to use up valuable fossil fuel resources.

* When **sewage** is properly treated, it can be recycled to provide an effective **fertilizer**. The large amounts of **water** used to carry away the sewage, and which would otherwise be wasted, **can be purified** even to the extent that it can be returned to drinking water supplies!

Points to remember

* Be sure that you know exactly what the harmful substances in tobacco smoke are, and the effect of each one.

* Learn the characteristic features of **viruses, bacteria** and **fungi**.

* Know that energy flows through a food web and is used by each member of the web for metabolic purposes. It is never recycled.

* Learn that energy is never 'manufactured', or 'made' (except by the Sun) – it is **released** by respiration.

* Know the difference between a pyramid of numbers and a pyramid of biomass. Make sure you know the difference between nitrification, denitrification and nitrogen fixation.

* Make sure you are clear about the difference between pollution due to use of fertilisers and pollution due to the use of pesticides.

* Be able to name the 'greenhouse gases' and know how they may be responsible for global temperature rise.

* Know the ways in which air and water can be polluted.

Exam-style questions for you to try

1. With which type of organism do all food chains begin?

    A. carnivore

    B. decomposer

    C. herbivore

    D. producer

2. The diagram shows a food chain.

    Which will be represented by the smallest block in a pyramid of numbers?

    A. bird of prey

    B. insect larva

    C. small bird

    D. tree

3. For the food chain shown in Q2, which of the organisms will be represented by the smallest block in a pyramid of biomass?

    A. bird of prey

    B. insect larva

    C. small bird

    D. tree

4. During the manufacture of yoghurt, which type of organism is used, and which chemical does it produce?

	type of organism	chemical produced
A	bacterium	lactic acid
B	fungus	hydrochloric acid
C	virus	glucose
D	yeast	alcohol

5. What is the cause of malaria?

    A. a female *Anopheles*

    B. a male *Anopheles*

    C. a single-celled organism

    D. stagnant water

6. Over a period of several months, a student recorded some activities of the wild life in a particular habitat. The following observations appeared in her notebook.

1. Young shoots of a crop of bean plants covered with greenflies (aphids) sucking food from the stems.
2. Saw a large bird (hawk), which usually catches mice, swoop to take a small yellow bird clinging to a bean stem. Noticed that these small birds often visit the bean field to eat some of the aphids or butterflies.
3. Flowers of beans being visited by many different species of butterfly.
4. Mice seen nibbling at some dispersed bean seeds.
5. Spider's web constructed between two bean plants with five large black flies caught in it. Rotting body of a mouse nearby attracting similar flies.

   (a) Complete Figure 5.9 by filling in the names of the organisms to show the feeding relationships in this community.

[4]

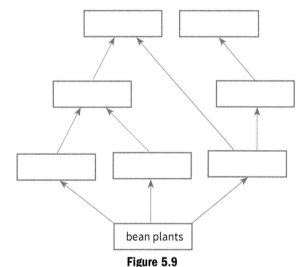

Figure 5.9

   (b) (i) What name is given to a chart of feeding relationships as shown in Figure 5.9?

   .... [1]

   (ii) Name two top carnivores observed by the student.

   1. ....

   2. .... [2]

(c) In each space below,

    (i) draw and label a pyramid of biomass for the hawks, mice and bean plants in this habitat.

[2]

    (ii) draw and label a pyramid of numbers for a bean plant, small birds and aphids.

[2]

Cambridge O Level Biology 5090 Paper 02 Q3 June 2008

7. **(a)** Define the term *drug*.

....

.... [3]

(b) Describe the possible effects of the abuse of a named drug.

....

....

....

....

....

....

....

....

.... [7]

Cambridge O Level Biology 5090 Paper 22 Q8 June 2011

Development of Organisms and the Continuity of Life

This chapter deals in detail with the way that life is handed on from one generation to the next. First it considers the process as it occurs in plants, and then how it occurs in human beings. There are detailed descriptions of the reproductive organs of both plants and humans, together with how humans can control the birth rate (and avoid sexually transmitted diseases). There follows a section on genetics and how genetics and the environment are responsible for variation and for the process of natural selection. The chapter ends with a consideration of some aspects of genetic engineering.

Reproduction

As organisms grow, they increase in the number of cells they possess. *Cells*, therefore, need to be able to reproduce. ***Each new cell must be able to carry out the functions of the cell from which it arose***. Therefore, each new cell must have the ***same genetic make-up*** as the cell that produced it. This is achieved by a controlled process of cell division known as ***mitosis***. In mitosis the cell's chromosomes first make exact copies of themselves (and therefore, also, of the genes they possess) and then the identical sets of chromosomes separate and each enters one of the two new cells produced.

Mitosis is therefore defined as *cell division that gives rise to genetically identical cells in which the chromosome number is maintained.*

Mitosis is responsible for making new cells during:

* growth
* replacing the cells that are damaged, and
* the cells that have become worn out.

Asexual reproduction

Asexual means 'without sex', and asexual reproduction involves the production of an offspring as the result of cells dividing by ***mitosis***.

Asexual reproduction is defined as *the production of genetically identical offspring from one parent.*

A population of organisms thus produced, and all genetically identical, is known as a **clone**.

The **advantages** to an organism of asexual reproduction are:

1. Only one parent organism is required.
2. It is a relatively certain method of reproduction.
3. Since the parent can survive in that particular habitat, the genetically identical offspring are bound to be suited to the environment as well.

The **disadvantages** are:

1. A lack of variation in offspring limits the process of evolution.
2. Adverse conditions and disease will be likely to affect all members of the population.
3. Overcrowding causes competition for resources (water, nutrients and, important in plants, light).
4. Distribution of the species is likely to be limited. However, asexual reproduction in **plants** is an important **commercial** process, since
   a. it produces **large numbers** of offspring
   b. it produces them **quickly**, and
   c. they are all of **known characteristics** (such as flavour, appearance, yield and disease resistance).

A commercial application of asexual reproduction in plants is the use of a technique called **tissue culture**.

Plants reproduced by this method of asexual reproduction include food plants (the **oil palm**, the **date palm** and the **banana**) and horticultural plants such as **Begonia**.

A method for reproducing plants, commercially using asexual reproduction

Method: Some actively dividing cells (e.g., from near the tip of a root, or from the **cambium** cells that lie between the xylem and phloem in the stem) are taken from the parent plant. These cells are placed on a **culture medium** in **many** separate dishes. The culture medium is a jelly-like substance called **agar** containing **plant growth hormones** and the ions necessary for healthy growth.

The dishes are kept in a suitable temperature and are covered to prevent the plants drying out.

Results: The cells continue to **divide** and then some of them become modified to produce small **(adventitious) roots** and some become modified to produce small **shoots** bearing **lateral buds**.

These plantlets can then be transferred to compost and will develop into clones of their parent. The commercial advantages are:

* It is quick.
* It is reliable.
* It gives plants of guaranteed type.
* It is profitable.

Make a list of plants with which you are familiar that reproduce using asexual reproduction.

Sexual reproduction

In sexual reproduction, two nuclei fuse together to form a new individual. Each of those nuclei must contain only **half** the full number of chromosomes for that species. (Each species has its own fixed number of chromosomes – which is 46 in the human, of which 23 come from the mother and 23 matching chromosomes from the father.)

In order to reduce the number of chromosomes by a half, those cells (known as **gametes**) that are used in the process are made by a special type of cell division know as **meiosis** (or 'reduction division'). Having the full number of chromosomes is described as the **diploid** condition; having half the number of chromosomes is described as the **haploid** condition.

Meiosis is therefore defined as *a reduction division in which the chromosome number is halved from diploid to haploid.*

A further advantage of meiosis is that, during the process, genes are 'shuffled' so that no two gametes possess identical sets of genes, thus **no two offspring will be genetically identical** (except in the special case of identical twins). (See the section on 'variation'.)

Sexual reproduction is defined as *the fusion of haploid nuclei to form a diploid zygote and the production of genetically dissimilar offspring.*

Sexual reproduction in plants

The *flowers* of plants are the organs of sexual reproduction. Flowers have the following parts:

1. The *sepals* are (usually) green, leaf-like structures which protect the flower when it is in bud.
2. The *petals* may be large, colourful, scented with lines on them (nectar guides) if the flower is pollinated by insects, but small, green or even absent entirely if the flower is wind pollinated.
3. The *anthers* are situated at the end of *filaments* (anther + filament = *stamen*). They contain *pollen sacs*, which make and then release *pollen grains*, each of which contains the *male* gamete(s).
4. The *carpels* are the *female* part of the flower. Each carpel is made up of a (sticky) *stigma* (for receiving pollen during pollination), connected by a *style* to the *ovary*, in which lie the *ovules*, which contain the female gamete.

NOTE

Pollen grains are **not** the male gametes. They **contain** the male gametes.

NOTE

It is still **sexual** reproduction, even though pollination may occur within the same flower or plant. It still involves the fusion of gametes – all of which will be genetically unique.

Pollination is the *transfer of pollen from an anther to a stigma.*

This may be *self*-pollination when the anther and stigma are either in the same flower, or in different flowers *on the same plant*.

Or it may be *cross*-pollination when the anther and stigma are in flowers on *different plants of the same species.*

Pollination may be brought about using different *agents* for carrying the pollen. The two most common are *wind* and *insect*. Wind- and insect-pollinated flowers show structural differences which are adaptations to their method of pollination.

The differences between wind- and insect-pollinated flowers

	wind-pollinated	insect-pollinated
petals	small or absent	large (to act as landing platform for insects)
	drab	colourful
	no scent	scented
	nectar guides absent	nectar guides present
	nectar absent	nectar present to attract insects

	wind-pollinated	insect-pollinated
pollen grains	small	larger
	dry and dusty	sticky
	smooth-coated	rough-coated
	light	relatively heavy
	more easily carried by wind	more easily carried by insects
	vast quantities (greater wastage)	smaller quantities (much more certain)
anthers	held outside the flower in the wind	protected within the flower where insects will touch them
	relatively large	relatively small
stigmas	large surface area	smaller surface area
	outside flower	inside flower

Examples of **wind**-pollinated flowers: **maize** and **grasses** (see Figure 6.1).

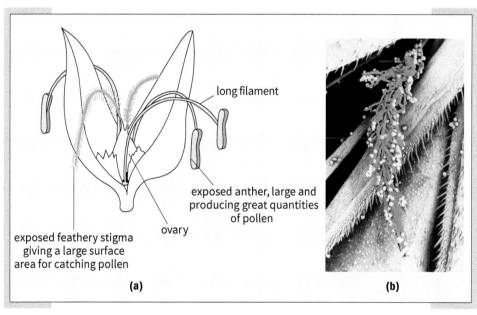

NOTE

When pollen from wind-pollinated plants is breathed in, the human body can 'mistake' the foreign chemicals on the coat of the pollen grains for potentially harmful pathogens. The result is that they cause a reaction similar to that experienced when a virus for the common cold is inhaled. This leads to a runny nose and sneezing – typical signs of 'hay fever'.

long filament

exposed anther, large and producing great quantities of pollen

ovary

exposed feathery stigma giving a large surface area for catching pollen

(a)

(b)

Figure 6.1(a) A wind-pollinated flower (grass flower)
(b) Pollen grains of a wind-pollinated plant on a stigma

See 'Hints' at the front of the book on how to draw the parts of an insect-pollinated flower.

Examples of **insect**-pollinated flowers: **beans** and **black-eyed Susan** (See Figure 6.2).

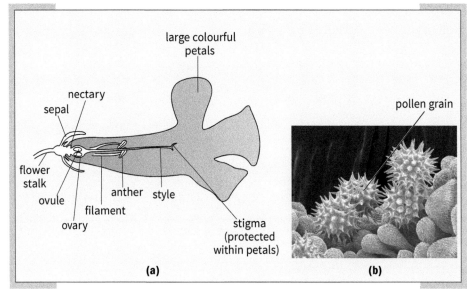

Figure 6.2(a) An insect-pollinated flower (black-eyed Susan)
(b) Pollen grains of an insect-pollinated plant on a stigma

*Using a large insect-pollinated flower, **carefully** remove the sepals, petals and stamens. Depending on the size of the flower, you may be able to remove the parts quite easily using your fingers, otherwise you may find a pair of forceps helpful.*

***Using a magnifying glass (×8 or ×10) make large drawings of one** of each of **the type of structure** you have **removed**. Also, make a **large drawing of the carpel** still attached to the flower stalk.*

***Use a hand lens to identify the structural features of a wind-pollinated flower (e.g., a grass).** Check against the list of differences between insect- and wind-pollinated flowers above to see how many of the differences you can observe in your two flowers.*

Using two clean glass slides, gently tap a mature anther from the insect-pollinated flower on one slide, and gently tap the entire wind-pollinated flower on the other slide. View both under the microscope (the use of low power will probably be sufficient). Compare the appearance of the pollen grains from the two different types of flower.

Fertilisation in flowering plants

When the pollen grain arrives on the stigma of the correct species of plant, a sugary solution on the stigma forms a medium in which the pollen grain will **germinate**.

Germination of the pollen grain involves the growth of a **pollen tube**, which releases **enzymes** at its tip in order to **digest** the cells of the style beneath. In this way, the cells of the style are removed to allow the pollen tube to **grow** down the **style** towards the **ovary**.

On arrival at the ovary, the end of the pollen tube enters an **ovule** through a small hole called the **micropyle**. Inside the ovule is the **embryo sac**, which contains the female **gamete**, within which is the female **nucleus**.

The end of the pollen tube then bursts to release the **male** gamete, which has travelled down the pollen tube from the pollen grain. **Fertilisation** occurs as the **nuclei of the male and female gametes fuse**.

Signs of successful fertilisation are the loss of the petals and, often, the sepals; the withering of the anthers and the rapid increase in size of the ovary – or ovaries.

The development of the fruit

Once fertilisation has occurred, the ovule is then called a **seed**. The ovary wall then becomes the **pericarp**, and the (**protective**) pericarp with the seed (or seeds) inside is called the **fruit**.

Seed structure

Sugars and amino acids arrive via the phloem of the parent plant, and enter the seed. Sugars are converted to starch (and, in some cases such as the sunflower, sugars are converted to fat). Amino acids are converted to protein. **Starch** and **protein** are then **stored** in seeds of dicotyledonous plants in two large storage organs called **cotyledons**. As shown in Figure 6.3, between the two cotyledons lie the **plumule** (or young shoot) and the **radicle** (young root) of the embryo plant. The **embryo** within the seed of a dicotyledonous plant is thus made up of **cotyledons, plumule** and **radicle**. The embryo is protected within a seed coat or **testa**.

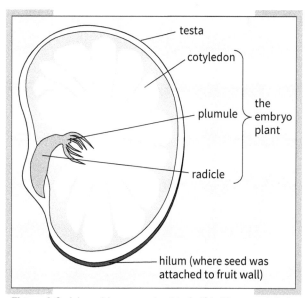

Figure 6.3 A broad bean seed cut in half (with one cotyledon removed)

Seed dispersal

Once it has developed within the fruit, the seed containing the embryo plant must break free from the parent and be ***dispersed***. In this way, the plant species is able to ***colonise new areas***. This also ***prevents overcrowding*** and ***avoids competition*** with fellow offspring for light and for nutrients.

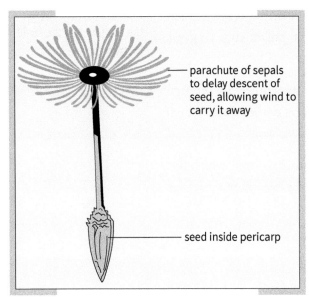

Figure 6.4 A wind-dispersed fruit

It may be some time before the seed is in a suitable environment for growth. The food stored in the cotyledons will keep it alive, though many seeds never find a suitable environment and there is great wastage. There are two main agents of dispersal responsible for carrying away the seed (often still part of a fruit and thus still inside its pericarp). These are ***wind*** and ***animals***.

Wind-dispersed seeds (or fruits) are usually:

* light in weight, and
* have their testa (if it is a seed) pericarp or sometimes the sepals (if it is a fruit) extended to provide a ***large surface area*** first to catch in the wind to pull the seed or fruit clear of the parent, and then to slow down its rate of fall allowing the wind to carry it some considerable distance away (See Figure 6.4.).

Animal-dispersed seeds (or fruits) (e.g. Figure 6.5):

* may rely on coloured, sweet and juicy pericarps around them to attract an animal (often a bird)
* may rely on enzyme-resistant testas so that the seed can pass through the intestines and leave the animal in the faeces at a distance from the parent plant, or
* may be dry, with hooks on their testas or on the surrounding pericarps, which catch a small mammal's fur and are carried some distance before being removed.

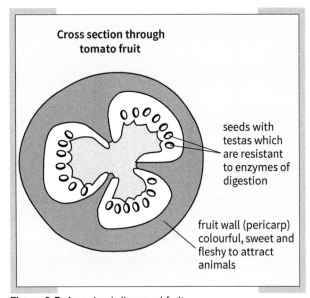

Figure 6.5 An animal-dispersed fruit

Germination of seeds

When suitable environmental conditions are available, the seed will **germinate**. The conditions necessary for seed germination are:

1. **water** (to activate the enzymes)
2. **oxygen** (to allow for the release of a great deal of energy from respiration to fuel the greatly increased growth rate)
3. a **suitable temperature** (enzymes operate efficiently only if the temperature is suitable for them).

Light is not necessary, except in a very few cases.

So long as conditions are suitable, the enzymes work to digest the food stored in the cotyledons (see section on enzymes in germination), which can then be carried to the **growing regions** of the embryo.

NOTE

Make sure that you do not confuse wind- and insect-pollination with wind and animal dispersal of seeds.

NOTE

It is scientifically more accurate to refer to water, oxygen and suitable temperature as the required conditions for germination than to say 'moisture, air and warmth'.

Aim: To demonstrate the conditions necessary for seed germination

Apparatus:
- four test-tubes
- cotton wool
- rubber bung
- ignition tube
- alkaline pyrogallol
- cotton, dry seeds (e.g., cress)

Method: Set up the experiment as shown in Figure 6.6, and leave the test-tubes for 2–4 days.

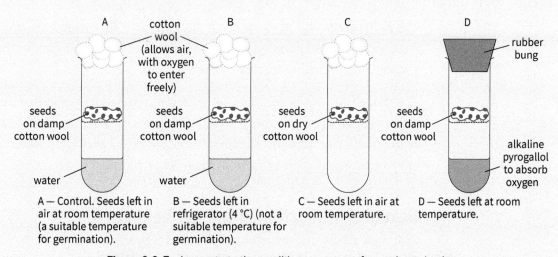

Figure 6.6 To demonstrate the conditions necessary for seed germination

Results: Only the seeds in the tube which has access to all the three conditions (tube A) will germinate. Thus a suitable temperature, water and oxygen are all necessary for germination.

The use of enzymes in the germination of seeds

Food is stored in seeds in the form of **large**, **insoluble**, **organic** molecules, either in **cotyledons**, or in a special storage tissue called **endosperm**. These large molecules are usually:

 * *carbohydrate* (often in the form of starch)
 * *protein*, and sometimes
 * *fat*.

When a seed germinates, these food stores must be changed into smaller molecules which can dissolve in the water which has been absorbed by the seed. They are then transported, **in solution**, to the **growing regions** of the seedling in order to make new cells.

Enzymes, present in the seeds, and activated by the absorbed water, bring about these chemical conversions.

substrate	enzyme	product
starch	amylase	glucose
protein	protease	amino acids
fats	lipase	fatty acids and glycerol

The **glucose** is used in respiration to provide the **energy** for the process of growth.

The **amino acids** are used to build up **proteins** in the **cytoplasm of the new cells**.

The **fatty acids** and **glycerol** recombine to form **fats** which are used as an energy store and to make important components of cell membranes. Fats also provide a considerable amount of **energy**.

The above enzymes, in common with many others, work by digesting the larger molecules. This is a process in which molecules of water are used to split (or **hydrolyse**) large **substrate** molecules into smaller **product** molecules. The enzymes are said to bring about **hydrolysis** of the larger molecules.

Sexual reproduction in human beings

Although a baby is born with a full set of reproductive organs, they are not functional during the first 12 (or so) years of life. Under the influence of **hormones** from the **pituitary** gland, the organs become active at the time known as **puberty**.

The male reproductive system

The male nuclei involved in the process of human sexual reproduction are located within male **gametes** (sex cells) called **sperms** (an abbreviation for spermatozoa). The male reproductive system is designed to manufacture sperms and to deliver them to the place where they will be able to fuse with a female nucleus.

Testes

(Singular – testis)

Testes are the **gonads** of the male; that is, they are the organs which produce the gametes – in this case the sperms. They are made of millions of tiny coiled tubes. The cells forming the walls of these tubes are constantly dividing first by mitosis, and finally by **meiosis** to produce up to 100 000 000 sperms per day. The testes work more efficiently at just below body temperature, thus testes are held outside the body in the **scrotum** (or scrotal sac).

Testes also begin to make and release the hormone **testosterone** at puberty. This hormone is responsible for **secondary sexual characteristics** of males. These are:

* the growth of hair on the face, under the arms and above the reproductive organs
* the increase in size of the larynx and the deepening of the voice
* the increase in strength of the muscles
* the increase in size of the testes and the penis
* the production of sperms.

Sperm ducts

Sperm ducts are tubes which carry the sperms away from the testes. They join with one another and with the tube bringing urine, at a position just under the bladder.

Prostate gland

The prostate gland is about the size of a golf ball, which surrounds the junction between the sperm ducts and the tube from the bladder. It manufactures and adds to the sperms a nutrient fluid (**seminal fluid**) in which the sperms are able to swim.

sperms   +   seminal fluid   =   **semen**

Urethra

The urethra is a tube that carries both urine and semen along the penis to be released from the body.

Penis

The penis is the organ for introducing sperms into the female. It contains spongy tissue which fills with blood to make the penis firm (an 'erection') so that it can more easily be guided into the female. These structural features are shown in Figure 6.7.

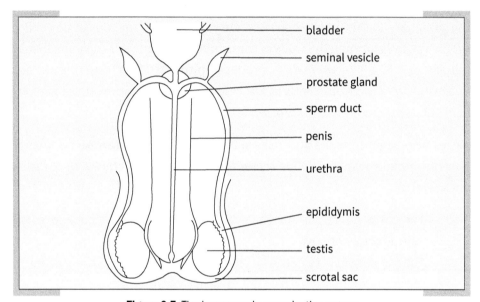

Figure 6.7 The human male reproductive organs

The female reproductive system

The female nuclei which are involved in the process of sexual reproduction are located in the female **gametes** called ova (singular – ovum). The function of the female reproductive system is to

* produce ova and to ensure that they are fertilised by the male gametes
* protect and nourish the embryo until it is born.

Ovaries

Ovaries are the female **gonads**, making and releasing the female gametes (ova). There are two, each a little smaller than a ping-pong ball, lying in the lower abdomen. The female releases one ovum every 4 weeks from alternate ovaries; that is, each ovary releases one ovum every 8 weeks.

The ovaries also release the hormones ***progesterone***, which maintains the spongy living of the uterus during pregnancy, and ***oestrogen***, which is responsible for the ***secondary sexual characteristics*** that develop at puberty and are:

* the widening of the hips to give support to a baby during pregnancy
* the growth of hair under the arms and above the reproductive organs
* the development of mammary glands (breasts)
* the development and release of ova (eggs)
* the onset of menstruation (the monthly period)
* the depositing of fat to give the body a more rounded figure.

Oviducts

Oviducts are the tubes which carry the ova away from the ovaries. They are lined with cilia which, together with a little muscular assistance, help to move the ova gently along. If fertilisation is to occur, it does so about ***one-third*** of the way along the oviduct.

Uterus

This is a pear-shaped organ lying behind and slightly above the bladder. Its walls contain ***involuntary muscle*** (i.e. muscle that cannot be consciously controlled). It is where the embryo develops during ***pregnancy***.

Cervix

This is the 'neck' of the uterus, where the uterus joins the vagina. It supplies mucus to the vagina.

Vagina

The vagina is the part of the female system which receives the penis during ***copulation***. It is muscular and stretchable (it forms part of the birth canal) and it connects the cervix with the slit-like ***vulva*** opening to the outside. The main features of the female reproductive system are shown in Figure 6.8.

NOTE

See 'How air is cleaned before entering the lungs' on p. 83.

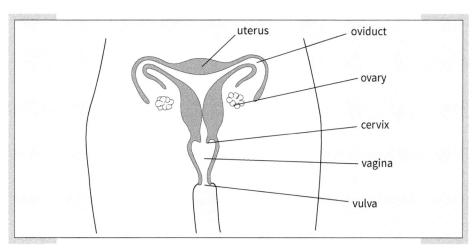

Figure 6.8 The human female reproductive organs

A comparison of male and female gametes is given in the table below and in Figure 6.9.

male gametes	female gametes
released in millions	released one at a time
able to move (are *motile*)	unable to move on their own
very small (0.05 mm – of which around 80% is tail)	comparatively large (0.1 mm in diameter)
very little cytoplasm	a lot of yolky cytoplasm
nucleus contains either an X or Y chromosome	nucleus always contains an X chromosome

NOTE

See later for more information on X and Y chromosomes.

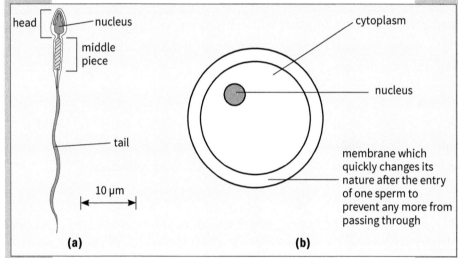

Figure 6.9(a) A human sperm
(b) A human ovum

The menstrual cycle

Once a female reaches puberty, she will start to *ovulate* (release ova from her ovaries). Ovulation is one stage in her *menstrual* or monthly cycle. This cycle is associated with the production of a *spongy lining* to the walls of the uterus in which the embryo will develop. As shown in Figure 6.10:

* Over a period of about 14 days, the walls of the female's uterus develop a *spongy lining* containing many blood capillaries.
* When the spongy lining is ready, ovulation occurs. The ovum passes down the oviduct, but if the ovum is not fertilised by a sperm, it continues its journey through the uterus and vagina and out of the vulva.
* The spongy lining then peels away from the uterus wall, damaging the blood capillaries, and is passed out of the vagina and vulva, together with blood. This is *menstruation* or the monthly period, which lasts for a few days, and occurs about 2 weeks after ovulation.

* Once the uterus wall has recovered, it begins to rebuild its spongy lining under the influence of **hormones** (See below). Meanwhile a new ovum is maturing in the ovary, again under hormonal influence. When mature, the ovum is released (ovulation), around 2 weeks after menstruation.

If an ovum is fertilised and the woman becomes pregnant, her menstrual cycle stops until after the baby is born. When a female reaches the **menopause**, usually around 50 years of age, she stops ovulating, and thus can now longer become pregnant.

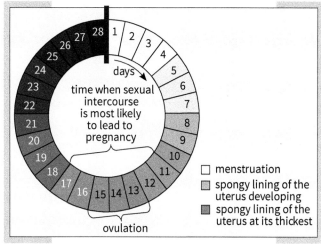

Figure 6.10 The human female menstrual cycle

Factors affecting the menstrual cycle

* **Stress** – At times of emotional stress, the menstrual cycle may become irregular.
* **Diet** – An inadequate diet can lead to an irregular cycle, and starvation can suppress the cycle completely.

Hormonal control of the menstrual cycle

The control of the menstrual cycle involves several hormones, some produced by the **pituitary gland** under the brain, and some by the **ovaries**.

The four significant hormones and their functions are as follows:

hormone	where produced	function
FSH	pituitary gland	promotes the ripening and release of eggs from the ovary
LH	pituitary gland	works with FSH to help ripen and release eggs, also prompts the ovary to release progesterone and oestrogen
oestrogen	ovary	helps to create spongy lining to uterus wall after menstruation and before ovulation
progesterone	ovary	secreted after ovulation to maintain the spongy lining to the uterus throughout pregnancy. It stops ovulation by inhibiting the release of FSH. The ovary ceases to produce progesterone if fertilisation does not occur.

The cells in the ovary that surround and nourish each egg before it is released (*follicle* cells) are the ones that become a temporary ductless gland after its release. This temporary ductless (or 'endocrine') gland is called the *yellow body* and, under stimulation from LH, releases *progesterone*. If fertilisation does not occur, the yellow body breaks down after about 2 weeks; thus, progesterone is no longer produced. The production of FSH is thus no longer inhibited so the cycle begins again.

Fertile and infertile phases of the menstrual cycle

When there is no ovum in the oviducts, fertilisation cannot occur. It is unlikely to occur if the ovum is not in the correct position in the oviduct, though this is affected by the fact that sperms can live in the oviduct for a few days, allowing the ovum chance to arrive. A woman's *most fertile* period is therefore *from a few days before ovulation* (allowing for the possible survival of sperms in the oviduct) *to a few days after ovulation*. Outside this time, she is less likely to become pregnant.

Human fertilisation

During copulation, sensitive cells near the end (glans) of the penis are the receptors for a *reflex* action leading to the release (*ejaculation*) of semen. The sperms are deposited near the cervix of the female, and then swim through the uterus and up the oviducts. If they meet an ovum, around one-third of its way from the ovary, *one* of the sperms will fuse with the ovum to form a *zygote*. This is the moment of *fertilisation*.

Development of the embryo

The zygote, a single cell formed from equal nuclear contributions from both parents, now begins to divide, eventually to form a *hollow ball of cells*. This stage in embryonic development is called the *blastocyst*.

At first the embryo absorbs nourishment secreted by the cells of the uterus, but it soon embeds itself (*implantation*) in the spongy lining of the uterus. Further division of the cells turn the blastocyst into a fetus. As shown in Figure 6.11, the *fetus* is surrounded by a membrane (the *amnion*) which forms the *amniotic sac* enclosing the fetus in a water bath (the *amniotic fluid*).

Functions of the amniotic fluid

* To protect the embryo from physical damage, e.g., if the mother falls over

* To support the embryo, keeping pressure even all round it, allowing organs to develop without restriction
* To allow the fetus some restricted movement.

The nutrition and excretion of the fetus

Both nutrition and excretion are carried out through a special structure called the **placenta**. This is made up partly of material from the fetus, and partly of material from the spongy lining of the uterus. In the placenta, blood in mother's capillaries runs very close to blood in the capillaries of the fetus. **Diffusion** of substances takes place between the two blood systems.

NOTE

The separate bloods **do not mix** – they may be different blood groups, and they would be of different pressures which would harm the fetus's developing circulatory system.

diffusing from mother to fetus	diffusing from fetus to mother
dissolved nutrients	nitrogenous waste
glucose	
amino acids	
ions	urea
vitamins	
water	
dissolved gases	
oxygen	carbon dioxide

The placenta is connected to the fetus by the **umbilical cord**, inside which run fetal blood vessels. The **umbilical vein** brings substances **to** the fetus, and the umbilical artery carries substances **from** the fetus.

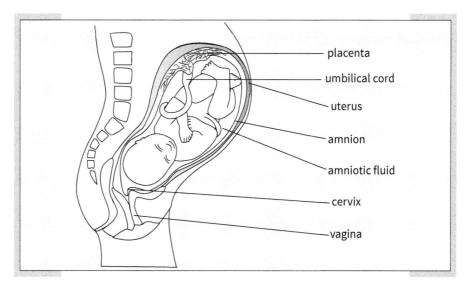

Figure 6.11 A fetus inside a pregnant woman

The dietary needs of a pregnant woman

An embryo's development depends on the food eaten by its mother, so a pregnant woman must adjust her diet accordingly. She should ensure that the levels of the following constituents are higher than in her normal intake:

* These should be raised to the approximate levels required by a very active woman who is not pregnant.

* ***protein*** * for the manufacture of embryonic tissues

* ***carbohydrate*** * for additional respiration in embryonic tissues

* ***vitamin C*** for making proteins in the embryo

* ***vitamin D*** and ***calcium*** for making bones and teeth of embryo

* ***iron*** for making embryo's blood.

The value of breast feeding

After the birth of the baby, ***milk*** from the ***mammary glands*** supplies the ideal food for the first months of development, since it

* is ***cheap***

* is ***readily available***

* contains ***all*** the necessary ***constituents***, in the ***correct proportions***

* is at the ***correct temperature***

* contains some ***antibodies*** which protect the baby against disease

* develops the mother/baby ***bond*** through breast feeding.

Some babies have suffered reactions to the substitute formula milk powders which are used in bottle feeding.

Birth control

The world population has risen alarmingly over the last few decades. It is already difficult to supply enough food to all areas of the world. A solution lies in ***birth control***. The main methods are discussed here.

The 'natural' or rhythm method

The rhythm method limits sexual intercourse (copulation) only to those times in the menstrual cycle when fertilisation is less likely. However, a woman's menstrual pattern may not be a reliable indicator of her fertility. Severe anxiety and malnutrition can suppress the menstrual cycle completely. Varying degrees of anxiety and dietary deficiency can lead to an erratic menstrual pattern.

Not all healthy and perfectly happy women have predictable and regular periods – particularly when **teenagers** or when approaching the **menopause** when eggs are no longer released. Often the most accurate prediction can only be that ovulation usually occurs somewhere between 12 days and 16 days before the start of menstruation. The rhythm method is therefore not a reliable method of avoiding pregnancy.

The chemical method

In the chemical method, chemicals that kill sperms (spermicides) are put into the vagina of the female before intercourse. This is not a very effective method of birth control when used on its own.

Mechanical methods

In mechanical methods, some form of **barrier** is put between the sperms and the ova. The barrier may take the form of

- a **condom**, a sheath placed over the penis before intercourse to catch the sperms when ejaculated

- a **femidom**, which lines the vagina of the female with the same result,

- a **diaphragm**, which fits over the cervix of the uterus, preventing the entry of sperms. It is usually used with a spermicide.

Barrier methods are popular and quite effective.

An **intra-uterine device** (IUD) is a contraceptive which is fitted inside the uterus. There is no barrier between the sperm and the ovum. It does not stop fertilisation, but it prevents implantation of the blastocyst. This is an effective method of birth control but it has to be fitted by a qualified person.

The hormonal method

The hormonal method is otherwise known as **the pill**. The woman takes a tablet which contains a hormone (similar to oestrogen and/or progesterone). When taken **regularly** the pill **prevents ovulation**; therefore, no ova are present to be fertilised. This is an effective method of birth control if the routine is followed carefully.

Surgical methods

* In the ***male***: Cutting the sperm ducts (the operation is called ***vasectomy***). It is effective but rarely reversible.
* In the ***female***: Tying the oviducts to prevent the passage of ova. It is effective and usually reversible.

Abstinence

Abstinence is another method of birth control. It involves not engaging in sexual intercourse except when intending to create a baby.

NOTE

It is inaccurate to refer to the HIV virus.

Sexually transmitted diseases

During the act of sexual intercourse, the bodies of the partners are brought into close contact during which ***pathogens*** can easily pass from one host to another. Sexually transmitted diseases (STDs, or sometimes referred to as STIs, where the I stands for Infections) include ***syphilis*** and AIDS.

Syphilis is caused by a ***bacterium***. AIDS is caused by HIV (the Human Immuno deficiency **Virus**). The table shows the features of syphilis.

disease	signs and symptoms	effects	treatment and control
syphilis	sores on penis, around vulva, slightly raised temperature, a rash, headache	destruction of the tissues of brain, skeleton, skin and other major organs	antibiotics, limitation to one sexual partner, use a condom

AIDS

The AIDS virus (HIV) lives in ***body fluids*** such as ***blood*** and ***semen***. It is thus transmitted from host to host when drug users ***share unsterilised needles*** to inject themselves, since there is usually a little blood from the previous user which is injected along with the drug into the second (and subsequent) user.

* It is transmitted in ***semen*** from one partner to the blood of another, if there is any tearing of tissues during intercourse.

* It is transmitted from an infected mother's blood to her baby's blood during the ***birth*** process.

* It may be accidentally transmitted in untreated blood during ***blood transfusion***.

Although drugs can slow the progress of the disease, there is, as yet, no cure for it. It can, however, be controlled by several measures:

1. ***Educating*** the public about how it is spread and what precautions can be taken.
2. ***Never*** sharing needles.
3. ***Avoiding sex with prostitutes*** since they are often carriers of the disease. Stay with one STD-free partner.
4. If in doubt, always ***use a condom*** or other barrier method of contraception which prevents direct contact between the body fluids of the two partners.
5. ***Treat*** all blood and blood products used in transfusions to destroy HIV.

Inheritance

Sexual reproduction leads to ***variation*** in the offspring. No two offspring from the same parents, produced by sexual reproduction, are genetically identical. An exception occurs when the offspring develop from the ***same ovum and sperm***, in which case they are 'identical twins'.

Two types of variation are seen:

1. ***continuous*** and
2. ***discontinuous***.

Continuous variation

Continuous variation is the result of the interaction of two factors:

* the genes that are inherited by an individual
* the effect of the environment on the individual.

The **environmental** factors involved might include

* the availability and type of food (in animals)
* disease and
* the climate
  * amount of sunlight
  * temperature
  * amount of available water
* the ions present in the soil (in plants)
* competition from other organisms in the environment.

In continuous variation, individuals show ***a range*** between the two extremes. Every possible intermediate between the two extremes will exist.

Examples of continuous variation:

* body mass
* height
* foot size.

Discontinuous variation

This is the result of **inheritance only**. There are **few** types, with **no** intermediates.

Examples of discontinuous variation:

* blood groups
* the ability to roll the tongue into a 'U' (either you can or you cannot!).

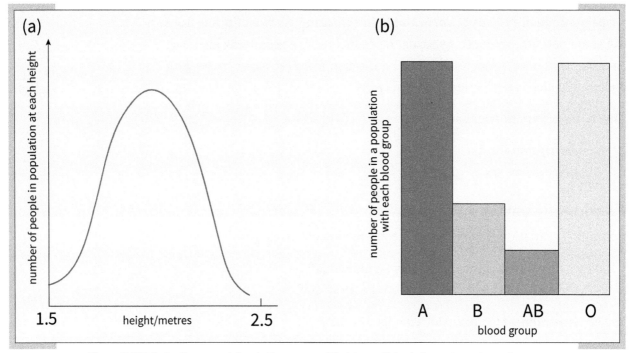

Figure 6.12(a) Continuous variation (with every possible intermediates between two extremes)
(b) Discontinuous variations (no intermediates)

The chemical structure of chromosomes

The Greek word 'helix' means a spiral.

Chromosomes, situated in the **nuclei** of all living cells (except bacteria which have no true nucleus), are made of the chemical substance **DNA**. The DNA molecule, looking rather like a very long, twisted rope ladder, is made up of two strands (of alternating sugar and phosphate units) held together by pairs of chemical units called **bases**. (These bases form the 'rungs' of the ladder.) The molecule is described as a **double helix**.

There are only **four** bases, but the sequence in which they occur in one of the two DNA strands is responsible for the sequence of amino acids in the protein molecules which are made in the cell. Since the sequence of bases on a DNA molecule is likely to be different for each (sexually produced) individual, it follows that no two individuals will make protein molecules with exactly the same sequence of amino acids.

The length of chromosome which contains the bases necessary to make one protein molecule is otherwise known as a gene.

The unit of inheritance

A **gene** is defined as *a unit of inheritance.*

Each **gene** is responsible for making **one particular protein** in a cell.

For the purposes of understanding the mechanism of inheritance, it is convenient to imagine a chromosome as a string of beads, like that shown in Figure 6.13. Each bead represents one gene.

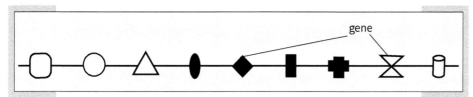

Figure 6.13 Representation of a chromosome

During cell division, genes are copied and these copies are passed on from parent to offspring, via chromosomes in the nuclei of the parents' **gametes**.

Genetic inheritance

Chromosomes in a healthy cell exist in matching pairs. E.g., humans have 23 matching (or **homologous**) pairs. Of each matching pair, one is inherited from a person's mother and one is inherited from their father. The genes on homologous chromosomes also match. Look at two strings of beads, like those shown in Figure 6.14. The order of the different shapes of beads is the same on both strings, i.e. the genes also exist in **matching pairs**. Matching genes on homologous chromosomes are called **alleles**.

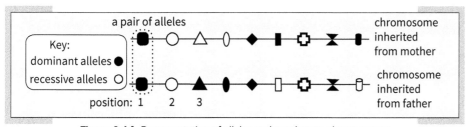

Figure 6.14 Representation of alleles on homologous chromosomes

Most features (**characters**) found in an individual are the result of the interaction between one allele inherited from the father, and one allele, occupying exactly the same position on the exactly matching (or **homologous**) chromosome, inherited from the mother.

A character(istic) which shows discontinuous variation will often exist in only two forms. The alleles that control it also exist in two forms, called **dominant** and **recessive**.

In Figure 6.14, the alleles in position 1 are both dominant, in position 2 they are both recessive and in position 3 there is one of each.

An offspring may therefore inherit

* **two dominant alleles**, one from each parent, and is then described as **homozygous dominant**
* **two recessive alleles**, one from each parent, and is then described as **homozygous recessive**
* **one dominant** and **one recessive** allele, and is then described as **heterozygous**.

These are the three possible **genotypes** of the individual.

If at least **one** dominant allele is present in the genotype, then the individual will show the dominant feature in their appearance (or **phenotype**). Thus the homozygous dominant and heterozygous genotypes will give the same phenotype. The homozygous recessive individual will have the alternative (or **contrasting**) phenotype.

Variation as a result of mutation

Genes and chromosomes are always subject to change (or **mutation**) as a result of environmental forces acting upon them. These forces are known as **mutagens**, and include

* **X-rays**
* **atomic radiation**
* **ultra-violet light** and
* some **chemicals**.

Exposure to higher doses of any of these mutagens will lead to a greater rate of mutation.

A **mutation** is *a spontaneous change in the structure of a gene or chromosome.*

Sickle-cell anaemia is an example of a condition caused by a **gene mutation**.

Both parents hand on a *mutated* (and recessive) allele for making *haemoglobin* in red blood cells. The homozygous recessive offspring cannot make effective haemoglobin, and cannot carry sufficient oxygen (and the red blood cells take on a distorted shape). A person with this condition is likely to die at an early age.

Down's syndrome is an example of a condition caused by a *chromosome mutation*.

There are 46 (23 pairs) of chromosomes in every normal cell of the human body (but there are 23 unpaired chromosomes in each gamete); 46 is known as the *diploid* number, and 23 as the *haploid* number.

If, in the cell divisions that produce the gametes in one of the parents, *one extra* chromosome enters one of the gametes, then there will be 24 (instead of 23) chromosomes in that gamete, and 47 (instead of 46) chromosomes in the zygote if this gamete is involved in the process of fertilisation. In older parents, there is a greater tendency for chromosome number 21 not to separate properly as gametes are being made. The child inheriting the extra chromosome will suffer from Down's syndrome, with consequent retarded physical and mental development, and characteristic facial appearance.

Monohybrid inheritance

Organisms inherit alleles for thousands of different contrasting characters. E.g., human hair is either curly or straight, and we either can or cannot smell the scent of certain flowers. If only *one pair* of contrasting characters, controlled in the individual by *one pair* of alleles is being considered, then this is described as *monohybrid inheritance*, of which there are two types:

1. with *complete dominance*
2. with *codominance*.

Inheritance with complete dominance

This is where the presence of only *one* dominant allele will decide the appearance (i.e. *phenotype*) of the individual.

Example: The colour of fur (coat colour) in mice

In mice, brown coat colour is dominant over grey coat colour. In an experiment, a *homozygous dominant* (or 'pure-breeding') *brown* male mouse mated with a *homozygous recessive* (also pure-breeding) *grey* female mouse. All their offspring (i.e. the F₁ or *first filial generation*) were found to be *brown*.

The offspring of the F_1 generation were then allowed to freely interbreed. It was found that their offspring (the F_2 generation) were brown to grey in a 3:1 ratio. This can be explained in a ***genetic diagram*** which must be set out as shown below.

Genetic diagrams

Genetic diagrams are a way of looking at the combinations of alleles that can be produced by two parents. In constructing genetic diagrams, the letters of the alphabet (rather than beads) are used to represent alleles. A dominant allele is represented by a capital (upper case) letter (like A, B or C) and its recessive allele is represented by a small or lower case version of the same letter (like a, b or c) as shown in Figure 6.15.

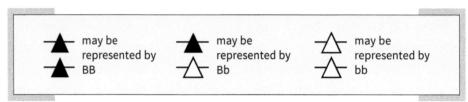

Figure 6.15 How letters are used to represent alleles

Full genetic diagram to show a cross between a homozygous brown-coated mouse and a homozygous grey-coated mouse

Key to alleles
- 'B' represents the dominant allele for **brown** coat colour in mice.
- 'b' represents the recessive allele for **grey** coat colour in mice.

Parents	male	×	female
genotypes:	BB		bb
phenotypes:	brown		grey
Alleles found in gametes:	B B		b b

(*Note:* Statistically, there is an exactly equal chance of either of the alleles from the male combining with either of the alleles from female at the time of fertilisation).

F_1 generation

Gametes		of the male	
		B	B
of the female	b	Bb	Bb
	b	Bb	Bb

genotype: all Bb
phenotype: brown

F_1 'selfed' (allowed to interbreed)   Bb   ×   Bb
gametes: B   b   B   b

(*Note:* Again, statistically, there is an exactly equal chance of either of the alleles from the male combining with either of the alleles from female at the time of fertilisation).

F_2 generation

Gametes		of the male	
		B	b
of the female	B	BB	Bb
	b	Bb	bb

possible genotype:	BB	Bb	Bb	bb
phenotype:	brown	brown	brown	grey
Ratio in a **large** sample:		3 brown	:	1 grey

The results are given as a statistical ratio in a *large* sample. The *smaller the sample*, the less likely that the ratios will be as shown.

In humans, where only one offspring is likely to be produced at a time, the *probability* of that offspring inheriting a particular feature is often given. Probability is usually expressed as a *percentage*.

Example: Cystic fibrosis in humans

Most people produce normal protein in the mucus found in their lungs. This is due to the possession of at least one dominant allele F. The homozygous recessive person has the genotype ff, and their lungs contain a particularly thick and sticky mucus, making gaseous exchange difficult. The person suffers from *cystic fibrosis*.

If two parents, both heterozygous for this condition (Ff) have a child, then the probability of this child having the genotype ff, and therefore suffering from cystic fibrosis, is 25%.

Gametes	F	f
F	FF	Ff
f	Ff	ff

The test (or back-) cross

Of the brown mice in the F$_2$ generation shown above, approximately one-third of them will be homozygous dominant (BB), and two-thirds will be heterozygous (Bb). There is no way of telling from their phenotype which type they are. Thus a *test (or back-) cross* is performed.

In a test cross, the individual is mated with a homozygous recessive partner.

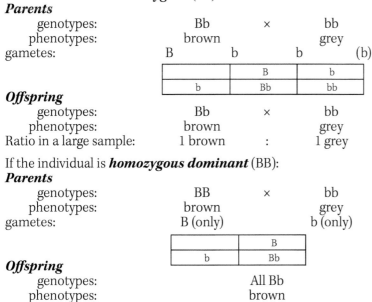

If the individual is *heterozygous* (Bb):
Parents

genotypes:	Bb	×	bb
phenotypes:	brown		grey
gametes:	B b		b (b)

	B	b
b	Bb	bb

Offspring

genotypes:	Bb	×	bb
phenotypes:	brown		grey
Ratio in a large sample:	1 brown	:	1 grey

If the individual is *homozygous dominant* (BB):
Parents

genotypes:	BB	×	bb
phenotypes:	brown		grey
gametes:	B (only)		b (only)

	B
b	Bb

Offspring

genotypes:	All Bb
phenotypes:	brown

Inheritance with codominance

Sometimes both alleles have an equal effect on the phenotype of an individual. When this happens, the alleles are said to be **codominant**. The individual which is heterozygous will therefore show a **third** phenotype – different from the two homozygous possibilities.

Example: The inheritance of human blood groups

This is still an example of monohybrid inheritance, but this time, there exist **three** possible alleles. Only **two** of them are possessed by any one person.

The alleles are I^A, I^B and I^o.

Both I^A and I^B are **dominant** over I^o, but are **codominant** to one another. Thus, the following possible genotype combinations with their blood group phenotypes are shown below:

genotype	phenotype
$I^A I^A$	blood group A
$I^A I^o$	blood group A
$I^B I^B$	blood group B
$I^B I^o$	blood group B
$I^o I^o$	blood group O
$I^A I^B$	blood group AB

An example of the inheritance of blood groups in humans can be shown in the following genetic diagram:

Parents

genotypes:	$I^A I^o$	×	$I^B I^o$
phenotypes:	group A		group B
gametes:	I^A I^o		I^B I^o

	I^A	I^o
I^B	$I^A I^B$	$I^B I^o$
I^o	$I^A I^o$	$I^o I^o$

Offspring

possible genotypes:	$I^A I^B$	$I^A I^o$	$I^B I^o$	$I^o I^o$
phenotypes:				
– blood groups	AB	A	B	O
– probability	25%	25%	25%	25%

Key terms

variation	the different characteristics produced in an individual by sexual reproduction
continuous variation	where both inherited and environmental factors determine the characteristics of an individual (e.g., body mass, height)
discontinuous variation	where inheritance **alone** determines the characteristics of an individual (e.g., blood group)
gene	a unit of inheritance, forming part of a chromosome, passed on from parent to offspring via chromosomes in the nuclei of the parents' gametes
gametes	male or female sex cells
alleles	different forms of the same gene
dominant alleles	the presence of a single dominant allele will have the same effect on the phenotype of an individual as the presence of an identical pair of them
recessive alleles	characters determined by these genes will not appear in an individual unless two recessive (no dominant) alleles are present
genotype	the genetic combination of an individual
homozygous dominant	individuals with two dominant alleles for a particular character, one from each parent
homozygous recessive	individuals with two recessive alleles for a particular character, one from each parent
heterozygous	individuals with two different alleles for a particular character
phenotype	an inherited feature in an individual's appearance. The homozygous dominant and heterozygous genotypes give the same phenotype. The homozygous recessive individual will have a contrasting phenotype.
mutation	a change in genes or chromosomes through environmental forces (mutagens), e.g., X-rays, atomic radiation
monohybrid inheritance	inheritance involving only one pair of alleles
complete dominance	when the presence of a single, dominant allele will have the same effect on the phenotype of an individual as the presence of an identical pair of them
codominance	when, in the heterozygous condition, both alleles have an effect on the phenotype of the individual

The inheritance of sex

Whether a child is born male or female is determined at the moment of fertilisation.

Of the 23 pairs of chromosomes in a human nucleus, **one** pair is known as the **sex** chromosomes. In the **female**, the sex chromosomes are **identical** and are called **X** chromosomes.

In the **male** they **do not** exactly **match** one-another. One of them is an **X** chromosome, exactly like those in the female, but the other is a (shorter) **Y** chromosome. Thus, the sex chromosomes are

> **XX** for a female, **XY** for a male

The **gametes** contain 23 **single** chromosomes, and thus only **one** of the two **sex chromosomes** that exist in normal body cells.

In **females, all gametes** contain an **X** chromosome (she has no other type to give).

In **males**, **50%** of the gametes contain an **X** chromosome and **50%** contain a **Y** chromosome.

Thus there is an exactly equal chance of the X chromosomes in the ovum fusing with an X carrying sperm to produce a daughter, or a Y carrying sperm to produce a son.

Parents
sex chromosomes
in body cells: father XY × mother XX
in gametes: X   Y   X (only)

At fertilisation:

	X	Y
X	XX	XY

Offspring

chromosomes:	XX	XY
	female	male
probability:	50%	50%

There is not only a wide variety of different animals and plants on the planet, but from the section on variation and genetics, it can be seen that there is a wide variety shown between members of the same species.

Examples of the variation shown by members of a population in a given habitat include:

* the shade of colour of a leaf-eating insect
* the sharpness of bird of prey's vision
* the speed at which a gazelle can run.

Selection

In all these examples, the variation can have some effect on the success or even on the chances of survival of that organism in its environment.

* The leaf insect with better camouflage may escape the notice of a hungry predator.
* The bird of prey with the sharper vision is more likely to find a meal – particularly important when food is scarce.
* The faster the gazelle can run, the more chance it has of escaping from a hungry lion.

All organisms are therefore in *competition* with other members of their species in that particular environment. The winners in that competition *survive to reproduce*. The losers provide food for predators, or fail to obtain enough food to remain alive.

It is the environment which 'decides' which organisms survive. The process is called *natural selection*.

Since the variation is controlled by the genes possessed by the organisms, the surviving individuals are able to hand on their advantages, via their genes, to the next generation.

Evolution

The offspring of the survivors also show variation, and so the process is repeated over *many generations*. By natural selection, lions will improve their stealth, and camouflage. Other species may now become threatened by the lion. Ecosystems are thus constantly in a state of change, and all organisms in it may also have to adapt to gradual climatic change as well.

This gradual change by natural selection is known as **evolution**. If, during the process, a population becomes separated into two isolated branches, each branch will then adapt to different environmental changes and evolve into **new species**.

Artificial selection

In the process of **artificial** selection, it is humans – not the environment – who perform the selection. That is, people deliberately choose to breed organisms with particular characteristics.

Many crop plants and farm animals of today are the result of selective breeding programmes. Examples include:

* increased milk production in goats or cows
* increased meat or wool production from sheep
* increased yield from cereals
* increased disease resistance in many crops.

As a result, greater profits are made from greater quantities of better quality produce.

In all cases, the following procedure is followed:

1. The individuals showing the quality required are selected.
2. Those individuals are used as breeding stock.
3. From their offspring, only those showing the desired quality **to the greatest** extent are selected.
4. These selected individuals are used for breeding.
5. This process is continued over many generations.

There is a danger, however, that this form of 'inbreeding', will increase the chances of two recessive alleles coming together. This may give rise to some form of genetically controlled deformity (e.g., a heart defect).

Genetic engineering

Since we are now able to identify specific genes (i.e. lengths of DNA which encode for the production of a certain protein), that gene can then be isolated and inserted into the cell of another organism.

Gene transfer

A particular gene, even when transferred to another cell, will continue to operate as it would do in its original cell. Thus, it is possible to cause a cell to produce proteins of a type which it would not normally produce, by introducing genes from other cells. In this way, genes for disease resistance existing in a crop plant with low yield can be introduced into a crop plant with a high yield, but low disease resistance. A person who inherits a genetically controlled condition like cystic fibrosis may be able to benefit by the introduction of genes from a healthy person. In both these examples, gene transfer is between organisms of the *same* species.

Gene transfer between organisms of *different* species is commonly used as in the production of the hormone insulin.

Commercial manufacture of insulin using genetic engineering

The gene for the production of human insulin (a protein) may be taken from a healthy person and inserted into a *bacterial cell*. The human DNA operates within the bacterial cell just as if it was in a human cell, and causes the cytoplasm of the bacterium to manufacture insulin.

The process of gene transfer is carried out as follows:

* The gene for insulin production is 'cut' from the appropriate human chromosome that carries it. The DNA is broken precisely at the required points using enzymes known as *restriction enzymes*.
* A circle of DNA found in a bacterium (commonly a bacterium called *E. coli*), known as a *plasmid*, is 'cut' open – again using a restriction enzyme.
* The human insulin gene is inserted into the cut plasmid, and its ends are joined to the cut surface, this time using enzymes called *ligases*.

The 'genetically engineered' bacterium is then given optimum conditions for growth and reproduction (using a vat, similar to a fermenter, at a suitable temperature and containing a suitable substrate solution on which the bacteria can feed). The genes in the bacterial DNA not only manufacture all the proteins that the bacterium requires for reproduction and growth, but *also the hormone insulin*.

After a period of time, the solution (which contains the insulin) and the bacteria are separated, and the insulin is purified.

In this process, the plasmids are referred to as *vectors* and the process of insertion of the gene into the plasmid as *gene splicing* (Figure 6.16.).

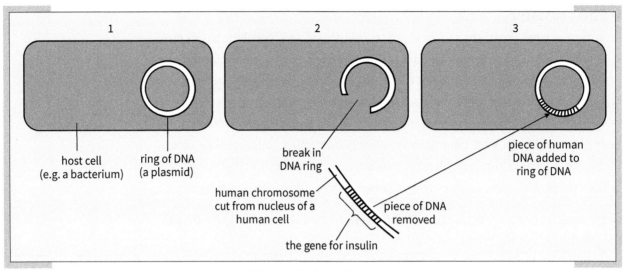

Figure 6.16 Gene splicing

The advantages of using this method of insulin production are:

* No animals are hurt during the process.
* A large amount of insulin can be harvested.
* The insulin is human insulin and not the insulin of another mammal.
* It is a relatively quick process.

Some advantages of genetic engineering

1. Chemicals with medical applications may be made cheaply and on a large scale, e.g., insulin, growth hormones.
2. Defective genes may be replaced with normal ones (as in the treatment of ***cystic fibrosis***).
3. Disease resistance (and resistance to herbicides) may be introduced into crop plants.
4. If a particular form of the gene which controls ripening is introduced into fruit and vegetables, they can be displayed for longer in shops before they go rotten.
5. The enzyme ***rennin***, used in cheese-making, may be made using genetic engineering, and not extracted from the stomachs of calves, thus making the cheese acceptable to vegetarians.
6. Cures for diseases may be found where none at present exist.
7. Disease-resistant crops avoid the need for pesticides and also avoid the pollution which pesticides cause.

Some possible dangers of genetic engineering

1. Genetically engineered organisms may become disease-causing and resistant to control measures.
2. Engineered genes from, say, crop plants may accidentally pass into closely related wild species.
3. The possibility arises that an organism (including a human) may be 'made to order', raising ethical arguments.

Points to remember

* Learn the advantages and the disadvantages of sexual and asexual reproduction.

* Know the structural features of a flower, and their functions.

* Know the difference between *pollination* and *fertilisation* in a flower.

* Be *absolutely certain* that you can distinguish between *pollination* and *fruit and seed dispersal* – particularly between *wind pollination* and *wind dispersal*.

* Know the names and functions of the parts of the human male and female reproductive systems.

* Learn the names and functions of the hormones that control the menstrual cycle.

* Be sure that you can distinguish between the functions of an artery and the vein in the umbilical cord, and know what happens in the placenta (especially that the embryo's and mother's bloods do not mix).

* Know how to prevent STDs (STIs).

* Know the conditions necessary for germination of seeds.

* Learn the difference between the term, *gene* and *allele*.

* Make sure you know that the sex of a person is the result of the presence of X and Y *chromosomes*, not X and Y genes.

* Know the difference between *mitosis* and *meiosis*, and be able to spell both words.

* Know the difference between *genotype* and *phenotype* and between *homozygous* and *heterozygous*.

* Be able to draw a full genetic diagram, including the words *parents*, *gametes*, F_1 or *offspring*, F_2, and showing the expected ratios.

* Make sure you can distinguish between *continuous* and *discontinuous* variation, and that you can give examples of each.

* Know the difference between *natural selection* and *artificial selection*, and give examples of each.

* Be clear on how genes are transferred from one species to another during the process of *genetic engineering.*

Exam-style questions for you to try

1. What happens during sexual reproduction?

   A. two diploid gametes fuse to form a diploid zygote

   B. two diploid gametes fuse to form a haploid zygote

   C. two haploid gametes fuse to form a diploid zygote

   D. one haploid gamete and one diploid gamete fuse to form a diploid zygote

2. In a developing flower, where is the pollen grain found?

   A. anther

   B. filament

   C. ovary

   D. style

3. What process indicates the moment of pollination in a flowering plant?

   A. the entry of the pollen tube into the ovule

   B. the germination of a pollen tube

   C. the landing of a pollen grain on a stigma

   D. the release of pollen by a flower

4. If a heterozygous black-haired mammal breeds with a homozygous white-haired mammal of the same species, what percentage of the offspring will be homozygous dominant?

   A. 0

   B. 50

   C. 75

   D. 100

5. How many chromosomes are found in the body cells of a person with Down's syndrome?

    A. 47

    B. 46

    C. 24

    D. 23

6. Figure. 6.17 shows sections through two different flowers, A and B, that are found on the same plant. One flower is male, the other is female

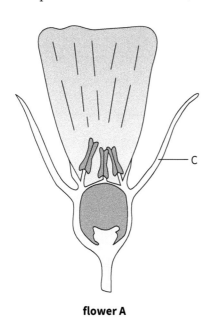

flower A

Figure 6.17

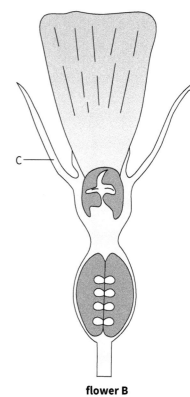

flower B

(a) Identify C on Figure. 6.17.

.... [1]

(b) State which flower is the male flower and give a reason.

    flower ....

    reason .... [1]

(c) (i) State the method of pollination in this plant and give two reasons for your answer.

Method of pollination .... [1]

Reasons i. ....

ii. .... [2]

(ii) State two other possible features, **not** visible on Figure 6.17, that are likely to be present in these flowers.

i. ....

ii. .... [2]

(d) In some species, plants with only male flowers occur while other plants have only female flowers. Explain the advantages of this to the species.

....

....

....

....

.... [3]

Cambridge O Level Biology 5090 Paper 2 Q1 June 2007

7. Some people are unable to smell the scented flowers of a certain species of plant. The ability to smell these flowers results from the possession of a dominant allele **M**.

Figure 6.18 represents a cross between a heterozygous father and a female who lacks the ability to smell the flowers.

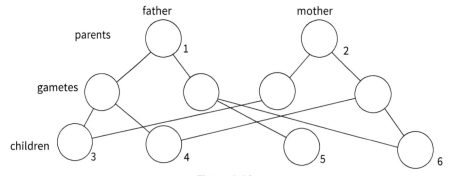

Figure 6.18

(a) In the circles, write the genotypes of the parents, the gametes and the children.

.... [3]

(b) State the proportion of the children that will be able to smell the flowers.

.... [1]

(c) Identify the people, numbered in the diagram, who are homozygous.

.... [1]

(d) One of the daughters who can smell the flowers eventually has several children with a man who has a genotype similar to her father. State the expected proportion of these children that will also be able to smell the flowers.

.... [1]

(e) State the results that would be obtained if the mother in Figure 6.18 was heterozygous and the father lacked the ability to smell the flowers.

.... [1]

For the exam-style questions with allocated marks, answers are provided in the form of a guide to marking your answers. The answers have been presented as a list of statements that could gain marks, but are not the complete answer. When you are checking your own answers, please note:

- *Where answers are given in bullet lists, each bullet point is worth a potential mark.*
- *There may sometimes be more than one way of making the scoring point. These alternatives are shown by an oblique line (/) or by the word OR. However, you can only give yourself one mark for each alternative.*
- *For some answers, there are more points for which you can get a mark than the total number of marks available for the question. For these, any combination of marking points is acceptable – up to that total number of marks.*
- *If a word is underlined, then that word should appear in the answer or you cannot give yourself the mark.*
- *If the statement includes AND, both parts of the statement should be included to give yourself a mark.*

Chapter 1

1 B

2 B

3 D

4 C

5 D

6 **(a)** nucleus, chloroplasts, membrane

3 marks

(b) vacuole OR ribosomes OR starch grains OR mitochondria or tonoplast

1 mark

(c) *(Although the good answer will describe the effect on the model **and** on a plant cell as water leaves them by osmosis, since the question asks for 'similarities' then mention of either the cell or the model would be acceptable. References to the cell have been used for this example.)*
- water would leave the plant cell
- by osmosis or diffusion
- because there is a higher water potential in the cell than there is in the solution outside / because there is a higher concentration of water molecules inside the cell than in the solution outside / because there is a lower water potential in the solution outside than in the plant cell / because there is a lower concentration of water molecules in the solution outside than in the cell / because there is a more concentrated solution outside than in the plant cell / because there is a more dilute (OR less concentrated) solution inside the cell than in the solution outside
- the cell OR cytoplasm OR protoplasm + shrinks, the pressure inside the cell decreases / the cell or model loses turgidity (OR firmness) / the cell becomes flaccid
- the tubing pulls away from the membrane / the cell membrane pulls away from the cell wall
- this results in a condition in cells called plasmolysis

- no sugar leaves the cell / sugar enters the space between the membrane and cell wall / sugar enters the space between the tubing and the permeable membrane

  6 marks maximum

7   **(a)** • it is the unit of life
  - it can undergo division / it is formed by division
  - it is a means of transferring genetic information
  - it is often incapable of independent existence
  - it can be modified to do many different jobs OR mention two different functions performed by cells
  - a cell contains a nucleus + cytoplasm + membrane
  - metabolic processes occur in cells (OR any one named metabolic process mentioned e.g. respiration)

  3 marks maximum

  (b) *(You will need to show that you understand the difference between a tissue and an organ and then to explain how these help to keep the blood circulating)*
  - muscle is a tissue
  - it is found in artery walls
  - where it maintains pressure of the blood
  - heart muscle is for pumping, it keeps the blood moving
  - nerves (in the heart) form a tissue
  - blood is a tissue for transport
  - blood vessels are tubes for blood
  - any two organs identified or named (e.g. heart / arteries / veins / any named blood vessels)

  7 marks maximum

Chapter 2

1   **A**

2   **C**

3   **B**

4   **D**

5   **D**

6   *(The question is not asking you to list nutritional components and their functions. It requires you to link your answers specifically to the nutritional components of the banana and the avocado)*
  (a) *(The value of each component must be mentioned before a mark can be scored.)*
  - carbohydrates are required for energy
  - low fat avoids obesity or circulatory disease
  - no cholesterol avoids circulatory disease
  - vitamin C is for avoiding scurvy (OR for good skin healing / avoiding bleeding gums)
  - fibre helps peristalsis OR helps to avoid constipation
  - calcium is for good (or strong) bones or teeth

- iron is needed for blood (OR for haemoglobin)
- protein is needed for growth / repair / enzyme production

4 marks maximum

(b) *(Again the deficient component must be linked to the effect of its deficiency.)*
- not enough protein for growth
- not enough calcium for bones or teeth
- not enough iron for blood OR for haemoglobin

3 marks

(c) *(The question asks for an explanation, so no mark is available just for naming the banana, but for explaining why it is better to eat before a race.)*
- the banana provides glucose
- for energy
- which is available more quickly than avocado
- avocado supplies more total energy
- but not so readily

3 marks maximum

7 **(a)** *(Note that the question asks about the distribution of chloroplasts – not simply about their function.)*
- there are no chloroplasts in the epidermis
- they are mostly in the palisade mesophyll
- and spongy mesophyll
- they are found near the leaf surface OR where they can most easily obtain most light
- chloroplasts can move within the cell to be nearer leaf surface
- they are present in guard cells
- that control the size of stomata

4 marks maximum

(b) • stomata allow carbon dioxide into the leaf
- for photosynthesis
- they allow oxygen to leave
- and water vapour to leave
- this helps to cool the leaf OR to bring water OR salts to the leaf

3 marks maximum

(c) *(Again, the question is asking about the position, not just about the function of the vascular bundles.)*
- vascular bundles form a network throughout the leaf OR form a central vein (midrib) OR they lie near the photosynthesising cells
- they help to prevent tearing of the leaf OR they are positioned to bring water / salts OR take away sugars
- xylem is strengthened / contains lignin
- forms a ring around the stem
- which gives support OR resists bending
- in the root it helps to anchor the plant

3 marks maximum

Chapter 3

1 A

2 A

3 D

4 C

5 B

6 *(Although the question refers to the 'uptake' of water by the plant material, since most of it is involved in the transpiration stream, then it is really a question on transpiration and the factors that affect it.)*

   (a) Bubble stops moving / remains stationary

   1 mark

   (b) • starts to move / moves
   • upwards / towards the leafy shootgradually

   2 marks

   (c) in either (i) or (ii):
   • it increases concentration gradient
   • around leaves / stomata
   • causing a faster rate of water loss / transpiration
   • by diffusion

   (i) • the moving air
   • takes away the vapour

   (ii) • there is a decrease in humidity / concentration of water vapour in the air
   • and removing the cover allows light to reach shoot

   (iii) • the stomata open
   • and allow water vapour to leave
   • there is also an increase in temperature
   • which causes a faster rate of evaporation

   8 marks maximum

7 *(This is not a question on how the heart works, it is about its role in making the blood flow round the body.)*

   (a) *(In view of the note above, you cannot simply describe the structure of the heart but need to relate it to the role in blood flow)*
   • valves in the heart
   • prevent backflow of blood
   • the heart has muscles that contract
   • the ventricles have thick walls / the ventricles have thick muscles / the ventricles contract powerfully OR strongly
   • to pump the blood / push the blood / squeeze the blood, the heart creates (OR the ventricles create) pressure in the blood system
   • the heart never tires or suffers from cramp / it is rhythmic / keeps going

   4 marks maximum

(b) • arteries always carry blood away from heart / arteries always carry blood under pressure
  • arteries are thick walled
  • arteries are muscular (OR have muscles)
  • they have a narrow lumen or central space
  • (the muscles) help to maintain pulse beat / allow recoil of the walls
  • arteries link to capillaries / veins

                                                                 3 marks maximum

(c) • veins return blood to the heart / veins have low pressure OR a large lumen
  • veins have valves
  • at intervals, to prevent backflow
  • they are thin-walled
  • (skeletal) muscles push the blood (e.g. the leg muscles push against the veins and that in turn pushes the blood up from one set of valves to the next)

                                                                  3 marks maximum

8 (a) • compound: sucrose / sugar OR carbohydrate (not glucose)
  • tissue: phloem

                                                                  2 marks maximum

(b) 2 marks for correct figures, and one mark for **both** units correctly expressed. 40 °C, 155 mg per g, (units)

                                                                  3 marks maximum

(c) • <u>glucose</u> (the correct sugar should be mentioned)
  • broken down or oxidised
  • water + CO_2 is produced
  • and lost to the atmosphere

                                                                  4 marks maximum

(d) • more starch or carbohydrate is made
  • by faster photosynthesis
  • there is a possible an increase in loss by translocation
  • there no change if photosynthesis was already at a maximum / or other limiting factors may be controlling the photosynthesis rate
  • no change in rate of loss by respiration OR respiration is not being affected by light intensity

                                                                  4 marks maximum

9 (a) P: hepatic portal vein
       Q: intestine / gut / alimentary canal

                                                                   2 marks maximum

(b) • nitrogen is not taken up or used by the body / cells / tissues / organs
  • nor released by the body / cells / tissues / organs

                                                                  2 marks maximum

(c) • haemoglobin
  • absorbs oxygen
  • which is not all released on one circulation

                                                                   3 marks

(d) • the names of the heart chambers (left and right atria + left and right ventricles)
 • in the correct sequence (right atrium - right ventricle - left atrium - left ventricle)
 • pulmonary artery (to the lungs) and pulmonary vein (from the lungs) both correctly mentioned
 • gas exchange occurs OR oxygen is absorbed and carbon dioxide is released
 • by the lungs OR by the alveoli

5 marks maximum

Chapter 4

1 B

2 D

3 C

4 C

5 D

6 A

7 (a) homeostasis

1 mark

 (b) • (C) receptor or sensor
  • detecting <u>changes</u> in <u>temperature</u>
  • (D) sensory neurone OR sensory nerve cell OR afferent neurone (*not nerve – as this is a collection of cells*) carries <u>impulses</u> (*not 'messages'*) to the CNS (OR central nervous system) OR brain OR spinal cord
  • carried impulses
  • to CNS (OR central nervous system) OR brain OR spinal cord

4 marks

 (c) *(You have first to consider the effect on the circulatory system of a cold environment, and thus realise that this would be the opposite of the effect on it of alcohol. Thus alcohol is working against the natural response of the body.)*
  • more blood
  • is carried to capillaries
  • which dilate OR get wider
  • blood carries heat
  • therefore more heat is lost
  • lowering the body temperature even more

3 marks maximum

8 *(Think carefully here that you are not confusing a hormone with an enzyme, or, perhaps, a drug.)*

   (a) *(Part (b) asks about a specific hormone, but this part asks about the meaning of a term. It would not be acceptable to describe the production and effect of a named hormone in this part)*

   - a hormone is a chemical
   - produced by a gland
   - that is carried by blood
   - affects target organ
   - is then destroyed by the liver

   4 marks maximum

   (b) • glucose is absorbed from the intestine / from a meal
   - causing an increased concentration in blood
   - insulin is released from islets
   - which are found in the pancreas
   - and it converts glucose to glycogen
   - which is then stored in liver
   - the permeability of cell membranes to glucose is increased by insulin
   - insulin secretion then decreases as glucose concentration drops

   6 marks maximum

9 **(a)** 15   (60 divided by 4)

   1 mark

   (b) • pressure decreasing
   - breathing in
   - external intercostal muscles contracting
   - diaphragm contracting
   - volume of thorax increasing
   - internal intercostal muscles
   - relaxing

   8 marks maximum

10 (a) ileum / small intestine

   1 mark maximum

   b) (i) any stated time between 36 and 52 minutes (*no mark without units*)
   (ii) 17.5 cm^3 per minute (*no marks without units*)

   2 marks

   (c) • water is lost
   - in sweat
   - less urine (is filtered OR produced)
   - curve rises later
   - peaks at lower figure
   - returns to original level sooner

   5 marks maximum

Chapter 5

1 D

2 D

3 A

4 A

5 C

6 (a)

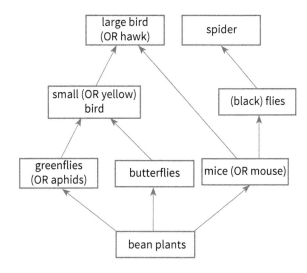

- greenflies (OR aphids) and butterflies can be either way round
- one mark for each correct line and one extra mark if all three lines are correct

4 marks

(b) (i) <u>food web</u>,

1 mark

(ii) • hawk OR large bird
- spider

2 marks

(c) (i) • correct *overall* shape (bean plants the widest and hawks the narrowest – the *exact* width of each block is not crucial)
     • all three levels correctly labelled as in the diagram below (large bird is an alternative to hawks)

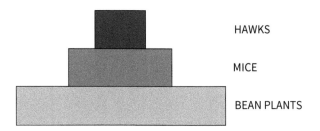

HAWKS

MICE

BEAN PLANTS

2 marks

(ii) • correct *overall* shape (the block for the bean plant must be the smallest and the block for aphids must be the widest)
     • all three levels correctly labelled (yellow birds and greenflies are acceptable alternatives to small birds and aphids)

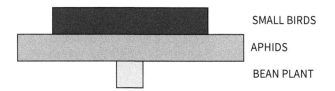

SMALL BIRDS

APHIDS

BEAN PLANT

2 marks

7 (a) *(It is important to know the definition of a 'drug'.)*
- externally administered OR taken
- chemical OR substance
- affects OR modifies OR alters
- metabolism OR chemical reaction in the body

3 marks maximum

(b) *(Heroin is referred to in the answer, but any drug of abuse would be acceptable.)*
- named drug (e.g. heroin)
- reason for taking it (e.g. creates a feeling of well-being)
- tolerance OR over time more has to be taken for the same effect
- dependence OR addiction / craving / cannot manage without it
- withdrawal symptoms – at least one described for the named drug (shaking / hallucination / diarrhoea)
- financial implications (e.g. expense to fund the habit)
- crime related to the drug (e.g. theft to buy more drug)
- effects on the family (e.g. neglect) OR on society (e.g. unreliability at work)
- adverse effect on health (e.g. weight loss / mental confusion – not 'death' as this can be caused by an adverse effect)

7 marks maximum

Chapter 6

1 **C**

2 **A**

3 **C**

4 **A**

5 **A**

6 **(a)** sepals OR calyx

1 mark

    (b) <u>flower</u> A AND presence of stamens or anthers *(it is not usually good practice to give negative answers, but in this case, credit can be given for stating that there are no named female parts e.g. 'no stigma')*

1 mark

    (c) (i) • insect

1 mark

          • short or protected filaments OR stamens OR anthers
          • protected stigma, large petals, (nectar) guides
          • stigma compact OR not feathery
          • petals form a landing platform

2 marks maximum

      (ii) *(This time, the question asks for 'positive' features, so we cannot accept 'no light pollen' etc.)*
          • any two from: scent, colour, nectar, pollen grains are rough OR pollen grains are sticky

2 marks maximum

    (d) *(This is really asking what the advantages are of cross-pollination over self-pollination. By examining the diagrams of the flowers, it is clear that self-pollination is not likely, and thus cross-pollination has to be employed by the plant.)*
    • cross-pollination must occur
    • alleles OR genes therefore come from two parents OR two plants
    • this causes greater variation (in offspring)
    • variation allows disease resistance OR colonisation of (OR adaptation to) a wider range of habitats
    • as a result of natural selection OR evolution

3 marks maximum

	Option 1					**Option 2**			
(a)	Mm		mm			mM		mm		1 mark

(a)

	Option 1					**Option 2**			
	Mm		mm			mM		mm		1 mark
	M m	m	m	OR	m	M	m	m		1 mark
	Mm	Mm	mm	mm		mm	mm	Mm	Mm	
	3	4	5	6		3	4	5	6	1 mark

(b) ½/ 50% / 2:2 / 1:1 / 1 out of 2   1 mark

(c) (Option 1) 2 + 5 + 6   OR (Option 2)   2 + 3 + 4   1 mark

(The option here must match the option 1 in (a) above)

(d) ¾ / 75% / 3 out of 4 / 3 smellers: 1 non-smeller (if you give the 3:1 ratio you must say which ones can smell or cannot smell)   1 mark

(e) same / similar / no change, or same correct answer as in (b)   1 mark

Glossary

ACCOMMODATION: The changing of the shape and therefore the focal length of the lens in the eye in order to focus on objects at different distances.

ACID RAIN: A dilute solution of acids that falls to earth when mainly oxides of nitrogen and sulphur in the atmosphere dissolve in rain.

ACTIVE SITE: Section on the surface of an enzyme where a substrate molecule fits exactly and is split into product molecules. The 'lock' in the 'lock and key hypothesis'.

ACTIVE TRANSPORT: An energy-consuming process where substances are transported through living membranes against a concentration gradient.

ADRENAL GLAND: Gland situated above the kidneys. Produces the hormone adrenaline.

ADRENALINE: Hormone produced by the adrenal glands that produces the body's response in times of fear or anger.

AEROBIC RESPIRATION: The release of relatively large amounts of energy by using oxygen to break down foodstuffs. Usually takes the form of the oxidation of glucose in the cytoplasm of living cells.

AIDS: Acquired immune deficiency syndrome. Caused by HIV, a virus that affects the body's ability to fight infection.

ALLELES: A pair of matching genes.

ALVEOLI (SINGULAR: ALVEOLUS): Air sacs of the lungs.

AMINO ACIDS: Simple, soluble units. A few linked together form a polypeptide; many linked together form a protein. Used in cells for building up proteins as the cells grow, and for making special proteins such as enzymes.

AMNION: Membrane that surrounds a developing fetus. It forms the amniotic sac, enclosing the fetus in amniotic fluid.

AMNIOTIC FLUID: A water bath that encloses a developing fetus.

AMYLASE: An enzyme that digests starch to sugars.

ANAEMIA: A lack of haemoglobin, often caused by low levels of iron in a person's diet.

ANAEROBIC RESPIRATION: The release of relatively small amounts of energy by the breakdown of food substances. Occurs in the absence of oxygen.

ANTAGONISTIC MUSCLES: Two muscles that provide opposing forces for movement. One of the pair contracts while, at the same time, the other relaxes.

ANTIBIOTICS: Drugs (e.g. penicillin) used to treat diseases caused by bacteria.

ANTIBODIES: Chemicals, produced by lymphocytes, that 'stick' to bacteria and clump them together, ready for ingestion by phagocytes.

ANTITOXINS: Types of antibodies produced by lymphocytes. They neutralise toxins in the blood.

ARTERY: Vessels with thick, muscular walls that carry blood, under high pressure, away from the heart. A large artery is called an aorta; a small one is called an arteriole.

ARTIFICIAL SELECTION: The deliberate breeding of organisms with particular characteristics.

ASEXUAL REPRODUCTION: The production of genetically identical offspring from one parent.

ATHEROMA: Fatty deposits that form on the walls of arteries, produced by a combination of saturated (animal) fats and cholesterol.

ATRIA (SINGULAR: ATRIUM): Two upper chambers of the heart that receive blood from the body and the lungs.

AUTOTROPHIC: Describes organisms (e.g. plants) able to produce their own food by using small molecules in the environment to build large organic molecules.

BACTERIA (SINGULAR: BACTERIUM): Unicellular organisms.

BALANCED DIET: Food and drink consumed by a person which has the correct amount of each constituent (e.g. proteins, carbohydrates) to enable them to be healthy.

BALL AND SOCKET JOINT: Type of joint which allows free movement in many planes (e.g. at the shoulder).

BENEDICT'S SOLUTION: Used to test for the presence of certain sugars including maltose and glucose (i.e. 'reducing' sugars).

BIRTH CONTROL: Methods of preventing pregnancy (e.g. through the use of contraceptives).

BIURET SOLUTIONS: Used to test for the presence of proteins.

BLASTOCYST: A stage in embryonic development after the zygote has divided to form a hollow ball of cells.

BLIND SPOT: The point in the eye where the retina is joined to the optic nerve. There are no rods or cones, so images formed here are not converted into impulses and relayed to the brain.

CAPILLARIES: Microscopic blood vessels that carry blood from arterioles to venules.

CAPILLARITY: The movement of liquids upward through very narrow tubes.

CARBOHYDRATE: Organic chemicals containing only the elements carbon, hydrogen and oxygen. Ratio of hydrogen atoms to oxygen atoms is always 2:1.

CARNIVORES: All consumers above the level of herbivore, i.e. all meat eaters.

CARPELS: The female parts of a flower – a stigma, connected by a style to the ovary, in which lie the ovules which contain the female gamete.

CATALYSTS: Particular chemicals that can affect how quickly chemical reactions occur (usually speed up reactions).

CELL MEMBRANE: Outer covering of the cell that controls the passage of substances into and out of the cell.

CELL WALL: A 'box' made of cellulose that encloses the plant cell – *not* present around animal cells.

CENTRAL NERVOUS SYSTEM (CNS): The body's coordinating centre, made up of the brain and the spinal cord. Receives information about the environment from receptors and directs a response to effectors (muscles or glands).

CHLOROPHYLL: A green pigment found within the chloroplasts of plant cells. Traps sunlight for use in the process of photosynthesis. Contains magnesium.

CHLOROPLASTS: Small bodies lying in the cytoplasm of those plant cells involved in photosynthesis. Green in colour because they contain chlorophyll.

CHROMOSOME: Possesses genes which are responsible for programming the cytoplasm to manufacture particular proteins.

CLONES: A population of organisms produced by asexual reproduction, and all genetically identical.

CLOT: A clump of blood cells trapped in a mesh of fibrin. It prevents the entry of bacteria at a wound. On the skin surface it dries and hardens to form a scab.

CNS: Central Nervous System.

CODOMINANCE: A type of monohybrid inheritance, when both alleles have an equal effect on the phenotype of the offspring.

COMPLETE DOMINANCE: When the presence of a single allele will have the same effect on the phenotype of an individual as the presence of an identical pair of alleles.

CONCENTRATION GRADIENT: When a region of (relatively) high concentration of molecules or particles is next to a region of (relatively) low concentration. Must be present for diffusion to occur.

CONES: Light-sensitive cells in the retina of the eye that provide a picture with greater detail and in colour. They convert light energy into electrical energy.

CONSUMER: Any organism which relies on the energy supplied by the producer in its food chain.

CONTINUOUS VARIATION: Where both inherited and environmental factors determine the characteristics of an individual (e.g. body mass, height).

CONTROL: Apparatus and materials identical to those in an experiment but lacking in the one feature being investigated. Used to make a comparison with the experiment in order to make the results of the experiment valid.

CORNEA: Transparent part of the eye that allows light rays to enter and refracts them towards each other.

CORONARY ARTERY: Vessel that supplies oxygenated blood to the heart muscle.

COTYLEDONS: Organs in seeds, often used for storing starch and protein.

CYTOPLASM: A jelly-like substance in which the chemical reactions of the cell take place.

DEAMINATION: Process by which excess amino acids are broken down in the liver to produce the excretory chemical urea.

DECOMPOSERS: Organisms which release enzymes to break down large molecules in dead organic matter into smaller ones which can then be recycled.

DEFICIENCY DISEASE: Conditions caused by a lack of a constituent (e.g. vitamin C, vitamin D, calcium or iron) in a person's diet.

DERMIS: Lower layer of skin containing most of the skin structures (e.g. sweat glands, venules, arterioles).

DETOXIFICATION: The removal and breakdown of toxins (e.g. alcohol) from the blood. A major function of the liver.

DIFFUSION: The movement of molecules from a region of higher concentration to a region of lower concentration, down a concentration gradient.

DISCONTINUOUS VARIATION: Where inheritance alone determines the characteristics of an individual (e.g. blood group).

DISSOLVE: Mix a substance into a liquid so that it is absorbed into the liquid.

DRUGS: Externally administered substances which modify or affect chemical reactions in the body.

ECOSYSTEM: A community of organisms living together in a habitat and connected through food webs.

ENZYMES: Biological catalysts that control chemical reactions in living organisms. Each has a specific shape and works most effectively at a particular temperature and pH.

ETHANOL: Alcohol used to test for the presence of fats. A waste product of anaerobic respiration in yeast.

EUTROPHICATION: The abundant growth of water plants. Accelerated when nitrate levels increase in waterways.

EVOLUTION: Gradual change in the characters of a species through natural selection. Takes place over many generations.

EXCRETION: The removal of waste products of metabolism from organisms.

EXPIRATION: The breathing out of air into the atmosphere.

EXTENSOR: One muscle in an antagonistic pair that contracts to straighten a limb at a joint. As it does so, the antagonistic flexor muscle relaxes.

EXTERNAL DIGESTION: Method of nutrition, characteristic of saprotrophs, by the release of enzymes onto an organic substrate ('food').

FATS: Insoluble organic molecules containing the elements carbon, hydrogen and oxygen only. Ratio of hydrogen to oxygen is much higher than 2 : 1. Formed by the joining of a glycerol molecule with fatty acid molecules.

FATTY ACIDS: Soluble molecules that, when joined with glycerol, form fat.

FERMENTATION: The anaerobic decomposition of some organic substances (e.g. of sugar to alcohol). Carbon dioxide is a waste product.

FETUS: A developing embryo in its mother's uterus.

FIBRIN: An insoluble, stringy protein formed by fibrinogen and enzymes released by damaged cells. It forms a mesh which traps blood cells and becomes a clot.

FIBRINOGEN: A soluble protein found in blood that plays a part in blood clotting.

FLACCID: Used to describe cells, tissues or organs when they lose their shape and firmness (turgor).

FLEXOR: One muscle in an antagonistic pair that contracts to bend a limb at the joint. At the same time, the extensor muscle relaxes.

FOLLICLE STIMULATING HORMONE (FSH): A hormone released by the pituitary gland that stimulates the ovaries to produce and release ova (eggs).

FOOD CHAIN: A sequence of organisms, starting with a photosynthesising organism (usually a green plant), through which energy is passed as one organism is eaten by the next in the sequence.

FOOD WEB: Interlinked food chains involving organisms within the same ecosystem.

FOVEA: A very sensitive part of the retina that has far more cones than rods. Also called the yellow spot.

FUNGI (SINGULAR: 'FUNGUS'): Parasitic or saprotrophic multicellular organisms that feed on organic matter by digesting and absorbing it. They do not photosynthesise.

GAMETES: Male or female sex cells.

GASEOUS EXCHANGE: The simultaneous absorption and release of gases by an organism. E.g., mesophyll cells in plants absorb carbon dioxide and release oxygen during photosynthesis; cells of the alveoli pass oxygen from the lungs into the blood and carbon dioxide in the opposite direction.

GENE: A unit of inheritance, part of a chromosome.

GENETIC ENGINEERING: Artificially changing the genetic make-up of cells.

GENOTYPE: Genetic combination of an individual. Three possibilities are: homozygous dominant, homozygous recessive, heterozygous.

GLYCEROL: Molecule that, when joined with fatty acids, forms fat.

GLYCOGEN: A carbohydrate with large, insoluble molecules. It is stored in the cells of the liver and muscles and in fungal cells. The conversion of glucose to glycogen takes place in the liver of mammals. This process is controlled by the hormone insulin, secreted by the pancreas.

GONADS: The organs which produce gametes (reproductive cells): the testes in males; ovaries in females.

HAEMOGLOBIN: Iron-containing pigment found in the cytoplasm of red blood cells. It carries oxygen around the body by combining with it in the lungs to become oxyhaemoglobin.

HERBIVORES: Consumers which feed directly on the producer in their food chain.

HETEROTROPHIC: Obtaining food requirements 'second-hand' either by eating plants, or by eating other animals which have eaten plants.

HETEROZYGOUS: Having a pair of dissimilar alleles for a particular character.

HIGH WATER POTENTIAL: Dilute solutions with a relatively large number of water molecules.

HINGE JOINT: Joint which allows movement in one plane only (e.g. at the elbow).

HIV: Human immunodeficiency virus.

HOMEOSTASIS: The maintenance of a constant internal environment in the body. Performed by organs of homeostasis (e.g. the skin).

HOMOZYGOUS: Having a pair of similar alleles for a particular character (e.g. both dominant, or both recessive).

HORMONE: A chemical substance, produced by a gland and carried by the blood, which alters the activity of one or more specific target organs. It is then destroyed in the liver.

HUMUS: Formed when dead organic matter decomposes in the soil. Humus provides a steady supply of ions. It acts as a sponge, soaking up and holding water in the soil, and helps to bind the soil together, preventing soil erosion.

HYDROLYSIS: Enzyme-controlled chemical reaction that involves the introduction of a water molecule in order to split a substrate molecule. The newly exposed ends of product molecules are 'sealed' so they will not re-join after being split, common in digestion.

HYPOTHALAMUS: The part of the brain responsible for monitoring changes in the blood.

INDUSTRIAL BIOTECHNOLOGY: The use of microorganisms in industrial processes.

INSOLUBLE: Unable to be mixed into and absorbed by a liquid (dissolved).

INSPIRATION: The taking in, or breathing in, of air from the atmosphere.

INSULIN: Hormone produced by the islets of Langerhans in the pancreas, involved in the uptake of glucose by cells and its conversion into glycogen.

IODINE SOLUTION: Used to show the presence of starch (by turning blue/black), also as a temporary stain for plant cells.

ION: A charged atom or group of atoms formed when a molecule dissolves in water (e.g. potassium nitrate dissolves to form potassium$^+$ and nitrate$^-$ ions).

IRIS: Part of the eye that controls the intensity of light falling on the retina. It has an antagonistic arrangement of circular and radial muscles.

IRON DEFICIENCY: Low levels of iron in a person's diet. Leads to a lack of haemoglobin, which is necessary for carrying oxygen around the body.

ISLETS OF LANGERHANS: Cells in the pancreas that produce insulin.

KIDNEY DIALYSIS: The use of a machine to perform the functions of a kidney. It removes chemicals with small molecules (urea, toxins and ions) from blood but does not allow larger molecules (e.g. plasma proteins) to leave.

LENS: Transparent, elastic part of the eye responsible for focusing an image on the retina.

LIGNIN: Chemical that helps to strengthen the walls of xylem vessels in plants.

LIMITING FACTORS: Particular factors that limit the rate of photosynthesis in plants, even when all other factors may be optimum. Examples are light, carbon dioxide, water and temperature.

LIPASE: An enzyme that digests fats to fatty acids and glycerol.

LIPIDS: Organic chemicals including fats and oils. Stored in special storage cells in the skin and around the kidneys.

LOW WATER POTENTIAL: Concentrated solutions with fewer water molecules.

LUTEINISING HORMONE (LH): A hormone released by the pituitary gland that stimulates the ovaries to produce ova. After the release of an ovum, it then stimulates the follicle cells in the ovary to produce the hormone progesterone. (Follicle cells were the cells that nourished the ovum during its development in the ovary.)

LYMPHATIC SYSTEM: A system of vessels for returning lymph (tissue fluid plus fats absorbed by the lacteals of the villi) to the blood system.

LYMPHOCYTES: A type of white blood cell, made in the lymph glands. They produce antitoxins and other antibodies which 'stick' to bacteria and clump them together for ingestion by phagocytes.

MAGNESIUM IONS: A form of magnesium absorbed by plants from the soil through the root hair.

MENOPAUSE: When a female stops ovulating and can no longer become pregnant. Usually occurs at around 50 years of age.

MENSTRUATION: Stage in the menstrual cycle when blood and the lining of the uterus are passed out of the vagina and vulva.

MESOPHYLL CELLS: Palisade and spongy cells in a leaf, involved in photosynthesis.

METABOLISM: All the chemical reactions occurring in cells.

MEIOSIS: (Also known as 'reduction division'). It is a form of cell division that occurs during gamete production, in which the chromosome number is halved (is changed from the diploid number to the haploid number). It also produces gametes that are all genetically unique.

MICROORGANISMS: Organisms so small that they can be studied only by using a microscope (e.g. viruses, bacteria and some fungi).

MILK TEETH: A person's first set of teeth that last for around 10–12 years, then are pushed out by the permanent teeth.

MITOSIS: A process of cell division when each chromosome forms an exact replica of itself. The two cells formed are identical to each other, and to the original cell.

MOLECULAR COHESION: The tendency for molecules to attract one another and thus stick together – particularly the case with water molecules.

MONOHYBRID INHERITANCE: Inheritance involving only one pair of contrasting alleles.

MULTICELLULAR: Living organisms that have many cells.

MUTATION: A spontaneous change in the structure of a gene or chromosome.

NATURAL SELECTION: The survival of those organisms most effectively adapted to their environment.

NEGATIVE FEEDBACK: A system which automatically brings about a correction in the body's internal environment (e.g. temperature), regardless which side of the optimum the change has occurred.

NEURONES: Individual nerve cells with their own cytoplasm, cell membrane and nucleus.

NITRATE ION: A form of nitrogen that plants absorb from the soil through root hairs.

NITROGEN FIXATION: Conversion of atmospheric (gaseous) nitrogen into nitrogen compounds which can be used by living organisms.

NUCLEUS: The part of the cell that controls its growth and development. It contains a number of chromosomes made of the chemical DNA.

OESTROGEN: A hormone released by the ovaries that is responsible for the development and maintenance of the female secondary sexual characteristics.

OPTIMUM: The best; particularly refers to a state (e.g. temperature, pH level) when processes can take place most efficiently.

ORGAN: Several tissues working together to produce a particular function.

ORGAN SYSTEM: A collection of different organs working together to perform a particular function.

ORGANISM: A collection of organ systems working together.

OSMOREGULATION: The maintenance of a constant concentration (e.g. of blood plasma, performed by the kidneys).

OSMOSIS: The passage of water molecules from a region of high water potential, to a region of lower water potential, through a partially permeable membrane.

OVA (SINGULAR: 'OVUM'): Female gametes produced in the ovaries.

OXYHAEMOGLOBIN: Constituent of red blood cells, formed by the combination of oxygen and haemoglobin.

PARASITE: An organism which obtains its food from another, usually larger living organism ('host'), the host always suffering in the relationship.

PATHOGEN: A disease-causing organism (e.g. virus, bacterium).

PENIS: Male organ for introducing sperms into the female.

PERICARP: Ovary wall that protects a fertilised plant seed. A pericarp with a seed(s) inside is a fruit.

PERISTALSIS: Waves of muscle contractions. Occurs in the oesophagus (pushing boli towards the stomach), and through the duodenum, ileum and colon (pushing food towards the rectum).

PHAGOCYTE: A type of white blood cell, made in the bone marrow. It has a lobed nucleus and is capable of movement. Its function is to ingest bacteria.

PHAGOCYTOSIS: The ingestion of potentially harmful bacteria by phagocytes. Prevents or helps to overcome infection.

PHENOTYPE: Inherited feature in an individual's appearance.

PHLOEM: Tissue for transporting sugars and amino acids within a plant.

PHOTOSYNTHESIS: A process performed by green plants, in which light energy is converted into chemical energy.

PLACENTA: A special structure which carries out the exchange between the mother and fetus of the chemicals involved in the fetus's nutrition, respiration and excretion.

PLASMA: Watery component of blood that carries dissolved chemicals, blood cells and heat.

PLASMID: A separate strand of DNA, often circular in shape, that occurs naturally in bacteria.

PLASMODIUM: A single-celled organism, parasitic in human blood, which causes malaria.

PLASMOLYSIS: When a cell's cytoplasm is pulled away from the cell wall as a result of osmosis. Occurs when the cell is placed in a solution of lower water potential, and water is drawn from the vacuole.

PLATELETS: Fragments of cells made in the bone marrow. They play a part in blood clotting and help to block holes in damaged capillary walls.

POLLEN TUBE: Structure produced by a germinating pollen grain. The pollen tube grows down the style towards the ovary by releasing enzymes at its tip to digest the cells of the style beneath.

POLLINATION: The transfer of pollen from an anther to a stigma.

POLYPEPTIDES: Formed by a few amino acids linked together. Enzymes in the body break down proteins to polypeptides, and polypeptides to amino acids.

PRIMARY CONSUMER: (also 'herbivore') A consumer which feeds directly on the producer in its food chain.

PRODUCERS: Organisms which manufacture and supply energy-rich foods, made by photosynthesis, to all organisms in their food chain.

PRODUCT: The molecules produced as a result of enzyme action on substrate molecules.

PROGESTERONE: A hormone produced by the follicle cells, after the release of an ovum, that maintains the spongy lining of the uterus and stops the pituitary gland producing FSH.

PROTEASE: An enzyme that digests proteins to amino acids.

PROTEINS: Contain the elements carbon, hydrogen, oxygen and nitrogen. Often contain other elements such as sulphur and phosphorus. Built up from amino acids.

PROTOPLASM: The cytoplasm and the nucleus of a cell.

PUBERTY: A stage in life when the release of hormones activates the reproductive organs. In humans, this occurs around the age of 12 years.

PYRAMID OF BIOMASS: A diagram constructed using the dry mass of organisms at each trophic level in a food web, with the producer at the base of the pyramid and the top consumer at the apex (top).

PYRAMID OF NUMBERS: A pyramid-shaped diagram composed of blocks similar to a pyramid of biomass but, this time, the width of each block indicates the number of organisms at each trophic level.

RBC: Red blood cell.

RECESSIVE GENES: Characters determined by these genes will not appear in an individual unless two recessive (i.e. no dominant) alleles are present.

RED BLOOD CELLS: Small, biconcave and flexible cells that carry oxygen around the body.

REDUCING SUGARS: A group of sugars, including maltose and glucose, that, when reacting with Benedict's solution, act as chemicals known as 'reducing agents'.

REFLEX: A fast, coordinated, automatic response to a specific stimulus.

RESPIRATION: The release of energy from food substances, that takes place in all living cells to perform all their functions.

RETINA: The innermost, light-sensitive layer of the eye.

RICKETS: A deficiency disease of bones caused by a lack of vitamin D in a person's diet.

RODS: Light-sensitive cells found in the retina of the eye. Important when light intensity is low. They convert light energy into electrical energy.

ROOT HAIR CELL: Plant cell specially adapted to absorb water and mineral ions (salts) from the soil.

ROOT PRESSURE: Created by the process of osmosis carrying water across the root to the vascular bundle of the stem. The pressure forces water into the xylem, and pushes it along the root towards the stem.

SAPROTROPH: Organism that feeds on dead organic matter through external digestion.

SCAB: A dried and hardened clot which covers a wound until the skin beneath has repaired.

SCURVY: A deficiency disease of the gums and skin caused by a lack of vitamin C in a person's diet.

SECONDARY CONSUMER: A consumer which feeds directly on the herbivore in its food chain.

SEMEN: Sperms and seminal fluid.

SEMINAL FLUID: A nutrient fluid in which sperms are able to swim.

SEX CHROMOSOMES: One pair of chromosomes that determine the sex of an offspring.

SEXUAL REPRODUCTION: The fusion of male and female nuclei to form a zygote. Zygotes develop into offspring genetically different from each other, and from their parents.

SPERM: An abbreviation for 'spermatozoon' – the male gamete (or sex cell).

STAMEN: The anther and filament of a flower, involved in the production of pollen grains.

STARCH: Insoluble carbohydrate produced by plant cells from glucose. Stored in the chloroplasts of photosynthesising cells and many storage organs of plants.

STOMATA (SINGULAR: STOMA): Pores through which gases diffuse into and out of a leaf.

SUBSTRATE: Molecule on which a catalyst works, changing it into product molecules. The 'key' in the 'lock and key hypothesis'. Also, the food on which organisms such as bacteria and fungi grow.

SYNAPSE: The gap between the dendrites (nerve endings) of neighbouring neurones.

TEMPERATURE REGULATION: Function performed by the skin to maintain body temperature, in humans, at 37°C. Includes sweating, dilation or constriction of arterioles, and the control of blood flow to the skin.

TENDON: A cord of connective tissue that attaches muscle to bone.

TERTIARY CONSUMER: A consumer which feeds directly on the secondary consumer in its food chain.

TESTOSTERONE: A hormone produced by the testes in males from the age of puberty. It controls the development and maintenance of secondary sexual characteristics.

TEST CROSS: A genetic cross involving one homozygous recessive parent.

TISSUE: Many similar cells working together and performing the same function.

TISSUE CULTURE: Commercial application of asexual reproduction in plants, in which pieces of tissue are removed from an organism and grown in an artificial medium in sterile conditions.

TISSUE FLUID: Blood without red blood cells, plasma proteins and some white blood cells. It bathes the body's cells.

TISSUE REJECTION: When the body's immune system fails to accept a transplanted organ (e.g. heart or kidney) and attempts to destroy it as a harmful protein.

TOLERANCE: The ability of an organism to take progressively increased dosages of a drug.

TOXINS: Poisons.

TRANSLOCATION: The movement of chemicals around a plant.

TRANSPIRATION: The evaporation of water from the mesophyll cells of a leaf, and the removal of that vapour through the stomata of the leaf.

TRANSPIRATION PULL: A force created by transpiration, where water is drawn up to the leaf to replace the water that has been lost.

TRANSPIRATION STREAM: A continuous stream of water and ions that travels up a plant.

TURGOR: The pressure created as water enters a plant cell, causing the cytoplasmic lining of the cell to press against the cell wall. Helps to make plant cells firm (turgid).

UMBILICAL CORD: Connection between placenta and fetus. The fetal blood vessels run within it.

UNICELLULAR: Made up of one cell only, as in the simplest living organisms.

UREA: A nitrogenous waste product which passes in the blood from the liver to the kidneys for excretion in urine.

URINE: Waste solution containing urea, ions, toxins and water.

VACUOLE: A large, central space in plant cells that contains cell sap, a solution made up mostly of sugars. Also called the 'sap vacuole'.

VASCULAR BUNDLES: Contain the tissues for transport within a plant – xylem (for carrying water and ions) and phloem (for carrying sugar and amino acids).

VEIN: Vessel which carries blood under low pressure towards the heart – thinner walls than arteries. A large vein is a vena cava; a small one is a venule.

VENTRICLES: Two lower chambers of the heart that pump blood out of the heart.

VILLI: Microscopic finger-like projections found on the walls of the ileum. Designed to maximize surface area to allow food absorption.

VIRUSES: Very small, parasitic organisms that cause disease. They cannot be treated with antibiotics. They do not possess all the characteristics of living organisms.

WILT: When a plant loses its rigidity as a result of a loss of turgidity in its cells. Occurs when the transpiration rate exceeds the rate that water can be absorbed from the soil, and water starts to be lost from the plant's cells.

WITHDRAWAL SYMPTOMS: Unpleasant effects that result when someone stops taking a drug to which they are addicted (e.g. heroin).

XYLEM VESSELS: Tube-like structures in plants specially adapted to conduct water and ions from the roots to the stem, leaves, flowers and fruits. Also provide support for the parts of the plant above the ground.

ZYGOTE: Formed by the fusion of male and female nuclei during sexual reproduction. Zygotes develop into offspring genetically different from each other, and from their parents.

Index